Reasons

for the

Seasons

Origins of the Christian Holidays

Jason Hunt, Th.D.

PublishAmerica
Baltimore

First printing

PublishAmerica has allowed this work to remain exactly as the author intended, verbatim, without editorial input.

Hardcover 978-1-4512-0017-1
Softcover 978-1-4489-5186-4
PUBLISHED BY PUBLISHAMERICA, LLLP
www.publishamerica.com
Baltimore

Printed in the United States of America

Introduction
My wife's womb was restored!

After having three children my wife Robyn began having miscarriages. We wanted to have a large family, but this set back was not only hard due to the loss of life- but the after effects on Robyn's physical condition. After the first miscarriage we went to the hospital, not really understanding the whole process; they explained it to us and then said they wanted to keep Robyn overnight to perform a "D&C"[1]. We waived the offer to stay and have the procedure done and they attempted to force her to stay, at which time we simply laughed and walked out for we know the Lord is our healer- we just needed some information to learn what to pray for- if you've read my first book *Divine Healing in the Kingdom*, you'll have a better understanding of our background and reasons for this.

After another week, she returned to normal and all was well. Several months later she conceived again, and a couple months into that pregnancy another miscarriage took place- we prayed, fasted, prophesied, but it still happened, but this time the bleeding continued way past the typical time frame. One Month, then two, then three, then four! Some may think that it's just ignorant not to go to the "doctor" to get checked out, but.they didn't have that luxury in New Testament times; either God healed or these things just went on (Luke 8:43-48), it's still like that today in 90% of the modern world, we just take it for granted here in the West.

So, we continued by faith; and during the fourth month we decided to begin celebrating the Biblical Holidays, as we were quickly coming upon Passover and needed to prepare. We had known of the Biblical Holidays for some time, but had not yet made the word come alive in our life, we knew that now was the time to act. We celebrated Passover and began preparing to celebrate the Feast of Unleavened Bread, it was the night before the feast, and it was during our scripture study that evening when Robyn shouted "I got it!" this is what she found:

Exodus 23:25-26 (NKJV): "So you shall serve the LORD your God, and He will bless your bread and your water. And I will take sickness away from the midst of you. No one shall suffer miscarriage or be barren in your land; I will fulfill the number of your days."

This is one of the promises God gave to those that kept the feasts (Ex. 23:14-24). It was then we knew that she would be healed- and four days into the Feast of Unleavened Bread, the bleeding stopped and she regained her health. Later, she again conceived, and again, in her fourth month, she had all the signs of another miscarriage. It scared us for a moment, so we became indignant and stood on the fact that God healed her during the Feast of Unleavened Bread. Heavy bleeding subsided a few days later which is when she was able to get another doctor's appointment. The doctor tried to affirm the worst as she could not locate a heartbeat or any evidence a baby was in the womb. So she left the room. Upon returning she asked Robyn if she would like a second exam with an ultra sound to which she agreed, and sure enough there it was- a baby. As I write this now, our son 'Daniel Asher' has just turned two years old.

In case you didn't pick up on the number four yet, let me reiterate- she bled 4 months, was healed on the 4th day of the Feast, then bled again on the 4th month after the Feast and this is our 4th child. The number 4 is the number of new creation— North, South, East, West; 4 Seasons; the 4th commandment is the first that refers to the earth (Remember the Sabbath). The 4th clause of the Lord's Prayer is the first that mentions the earth. The materials of the tabernacle were 4 and so were the coverings and the ornamentations. God has created a new thing in our lives and ministry; and it was this experience that gave us the confirmation we needed that the blessings of obeying the Word of the Lord regarding the celebration of His holidays over those created by man is for the church today- and should have never been changed!

Thus, my primary purpose in writing this text is to demonstrate the pervasive Pagan (anti-Christian) origins of the major and otherwise minor 'Christian' holidays of Easter, Christmas, St. Patrick's Day, St. Valentine's Day, New Years Day and Halloween as celebrated in the United States and much of the modern world, all of which were created by man. Secondly, I seek to bring to light the holidays of the Lord that we are to celebrate, along with several reasons why we should and are actually expected to do so.

I do not seek to muddy your spiritual water with a message of condemnation, but I seek to build you up through the truths revealed in the following pages only to get you to love Jesus more than the man made traditions we've entertained in our ignorance.

Hosea 4:6 states that God's people die due to a lack of knowledge, because they reject it; and because they reject it, He shall reject them from becoming His priests.

This is a prophetic picture of how Christians that blindly follow others will be rejected from being the Bride of Christ; for the Bride shall be pure and without blemish- basically the Bride will not mix true and false worship of God; and the Bride will keep the commandments of God and hold the testimony of Jesus Christ. The Bride shall be a royal priesthood and holy nation (Rev. 5, 1 Peter 2:9).

Plainly stated, to reject truth is to reject the Messiah Jesus himself for He is truth (John 14:6). As Christians, we are called to be set apart from the world of darkness (Eph. 5:11) and the traditions of men (Mark 7). To "learn not the way of the heathen" (Jer. 10:2); "Abstain from all appearance of evil." (1 Thessalonians 5:22), to name only a few! Why then do Christians contend against any teaching that plainly reveals the truth of the pagan nature of their beloved holidays?

In general, people fear and do not accept change, though they believe they want it... However, actions speak louder than words.

Common excuses among Christians range from "Well I didn't know", to "I know, but my church teaches this..." One author on 'Radical Church Reform' states *"Our spiritual forefathers chose to compete with the pagans by redeeming certain days for Jesus Christ that had traditionally been kept sacred by their heathen neighbors. The Christians chose those same days to honor their Lord instead of going along with the pagan celebrations. It was a testimony against paganism and a way to "redeem the days." I find nothing wrong with this at all."*[3]

This view is most commonly taught and accepted by the majority of churches today. However, this view is grossly flawed due to the fact that these "Christian forefathers" where not concerned with the Christianity preached by Jesus and the Apostles- they were only concerned with gaining power over the people. These supposed "Christian Forefathers" were all of a pagan Gentile background and where Anti-Semites (Anti-Jewish). The Christians were originally considered a sect of Judaism just like the Pharisees or Essences. It wasn't really until the Council of Nicaea that Christianity became an independent religion, and that was over 300 years after the resurrection. This Romanized Christianity took the same methods, symbolism, and dates of the old pagan festival days they had always celebrated and simply ascribed a saint's name to them in their effort to redeem them "for Christ".

Herein lays the problem, nothing changed but the title of the day! Additionally, you will find no Biblical precedent for the redeeming of days, nor will you find any mention of our supposedly redeemed 'Christian' holidays in the Bible.[2]

We hear so much today *"Keep Christ in Christmas"*, the thing is; Jesus never had anything to do with Christmas! So if holidays are not listed in the bible, shouldn't we stop trying to base them on biblical truth? When we look at the true nature, and often times the original name of the festival our Christian holiday supposedly redeemed, we find it throughout the scriptures with the command to rebuke, reprove and turn away from it, a name change isn't enough to justify a practice of a holiday dedicated to an idol.

This same author on "*Radical Church Reform*" further goes on to state "*How, why, and when God's people remember and celebrate the birth, death, and resurrection of Jesus Christ is a matter of personal conscience (Romans 14:1-6). Therefore, I have never had a burden to address these things. I stand with Paul, who was a non-legalist, in his conclusion about observing certain days: "Let every man be persuaded in his own mind."*[4]

Would it be okay for someone to celebrate your birthday whenever they chose? They didn't bother to ask you, and they left the celebration of your birth up to their personal conscience, they even had all their friends agree that they would celebrate your birth on a day they chose for you. They've convinced themselves that March is a better time to celebrate your September birthday... Then, when they do celebrate "your day", they buy gifts for themselves and their family, but not you... They have a party, but don't invite you and they decorate, but not with anything you appreciate or value. Does this make sense? Of course not, yet this is what over a billion people do every year in the name of "Christ". This is a plain illustration of using God's name in vain...

In regards to Romans 14:1-6, Paul was actually speaking about food and fasting; what to eat during those fast days etc. and not holidays in general. Paul stated that there was no difference regarding which Sabbath days we chose to fast on or what we chose to fast from, not one day is holier than another for fasting purposes. The area of concern was not judging the person who was not fasting when you where, and not eating what you where eating.

When to celebrate the birth, death and resurrection is clearly outlined in scripture and how to do so. So to leave it as a matter of "personal conscience" leads one to honor the idols they've created in their heart.

The Lord has made it clear; there is a way to worship Him and a way not to worship Him. It is my mission in this text to unveil the truth behind the history of our holidays, to unveil the pagan gods Christians are actually praising, and to give the Biblical record for holidays we Biblically commanded to celebrate, yes, even as Gentile Christians.

Jason Hunt
Bethlehem, Kentucky
During the Days of Awe 2009

Chapter 1
Pagan Origins

To the ordinary public or average Christian the connection between Paganism and Christianity still seems rather remote. Indeed the common notion is that Christianity was really a miraculous interposition into and dislocation of the old order of the world; that the pagan gods fled away in dismay before the sign of the Cross, and at the sound of the name of Jesus.

Doubtless this was a view much encouraged by the early Catholic Church itself—if only to enhance its own authority and importance; yet, as is well known to every serious Bible student, it is quite misleading and contrary to fact. The main Christian traditions and festivals, besides a great mass of affiliated legend and ceremony, are really quite directly derived from, and related to, preceding Nature worships; and it has only been by a good deal of deliberate mystification, romancing, and falsification that this derivation has been kept out of sight.[1]

At the time of the life of Jesus, and for some centuries before, the Mediterranean and neighboring world had been the scene of a vast number of pagan creeds and rituals. There were Temples without end dedicated to gods like Apollo or Dionysus among the Greeks, Hercules among the Romans, Mithras among the Persians and those Romans who had been stationed as soldiers throughout Persia and Arabia, Adonis and Attis in Syria and Phrygia, Osiris and Isis and Horus in Egypt, Baal and Astarte among the Babylonians and Carthaginians, and so forth. Societies, large or small, united believers and the devout in the service or ceremonials connected with their respective deities, and in the creeds which they confessed concerning these deities. And an extraordinarily interesting fact, for us, is that notwithstanding great geographical distances and racial differences between the adherents of these various cults, as well as differences in the details of their services, the general outlines of their creeds and ceremonials were—if not identical—so markedly similar it is amazing.

I cannot of course go at length into these different cults, but I may say roughly that of all or nearly all the deities above-mentioned it was said and believed that:

(1) They were born on or very near our Christmas Day.

(2) They were born of a Virgin-Mother.

(3) Birthed in a Cave or Underground Chamber.

(4) They led a life of toil for Mankind.

(5) And were called by the names of Light-bringer, Healer, Mediator, Savior, and Deliverer.

(6) They were however vanquished by the Powers of Darkness.

(7) And descended into Hell or an Underworld.

(8) They rose again from the dead, and became the pioneers of mankind to the Heavenly world.

(9) They founded Communions of Saints, and "Churches" or groups of followers into which disciples were received by various styles of Baptism.

(10) And they were commemorated by Festivals typically commemorating their birth as was pagan tradition.[2]

How is it possible that so many cultures spaced so far apart held such similar beliefs? The Tower of Babel... As you may recall, all people of the world spoke one language and knew of only one God at one time, that is, before they decided to build a tower. For when the Spirit of the Lord confused the languages of man, it caused men to separate to different areas of the land, thus resulting in different nations, tribes, people, and tongues. This is why the ancient people in Mexico have the same flood stories as those in Egypt and Persia. So, the same stories where utilized to create new religious systems and beliefs, all straying from what God intended.

For the sake of further understanding, allow me to give a few brief examples.

Mithras was born in a cave, on the 25th of December.[3] He was born of a Virgin.[4] He traveled far and wide as a teacher and illuminator of men. He slew the Divine Bull (symbol of the gross Earth which the sunlight fructifies). His great festivals were the winter solstice and the spring equinox (Christmas and Easter). He had twelve companions or disciples (the twelve months). He was buried in a tomb, from which he rose and his resurrection was celebrated yearly with great rejoicings. He was called Savior and Mediator, and sometimes figured as a Lamb; and sacramental feasts in remembrance of him were held by his followers. This legend is apparently partly astronomical and partly vegetational; and the same may be said of the following about Osiris.

Osiris was born (Plutarch tells us) on the 361st day of the year, the 27th of December. He too, like Mithras and Dionysus, was a great traveler. As King of Egypt he taught men civil arts, and "tamed them by music and gentleness, not by force of arms";[5] he was the discoverer of corn and wine. But he was betrayed by Typhon, the power of darkness, and slain and dismembered. "This happened," says Plutarch, "on the 17th of the month Athyr, when the sun enters into the Scorpion" (the sign of the Zodiac which indicates the oncoming of winter). His body was placed in a box, but afterwards, on the 19th, came again to life, and, as in the cults of Mithra, Dionysus, Adonis and others, so in the cult of Osiris, an image placed in a coffin was brought out before the worshipers and saluted with glad cries of "Osiris is risen."[6] "His sufferings, his death and his resurrection were enacted year by year in a great mystery-play at Abydos."[6](Much like the Passion plays of today)

The two following legends have more distinctly the character of Vegetation myths.

Adonis or Tammuz, the Syrian god of vegetation, was a very beautiful youth, born of a Virgin (Nature), and so beautiful that Venus and Proserpine (the goddesses of the Upper and Underworlds) both fell in love with him. To reconcile their claims it was agreed that he should spend half the year (summer) in the upper world and the winter half with Proserpine below. He was killed by a boar (Typhon) in the autumn. And every year the maidens "wept for Adonis" (see Ezekiel 8:14).

In the spring a festival of his resurrection was held—the women set out to seek him, and having found the supposed corpse placed it (a wooden image) in a coffin or hollow tree, and performed wild rites and lamentations, followed by even wilder rejoicings over his supposed resurrection. At Aphaca in the North of Syria, and halfway between Byblus and Baalbec, there was a famous grove and temple of Astarte (See Judges 6:25 {Astarte is the Greek spelling of Ashtaroth}), near which was a wild romantic gorge full of trees, the birthplace of a certain river Adonis—the water rushing from a Cavern, under lofty cliffs. Here (it was said) every year the youth Adonis was again wounded to death and the river ran red with his blood;[7] while the scarlet anemone bloomed among the cedars and walnuts.

The story of Attis is very similar. He was a fair young shepherd or herdsman of Phrygia, beloved by Cybele (or Demeter), the Mother of the gods. He was born of a Virgin —Nana—who conceived by putting a ripe almond or pomegranate in her bosom. He died, either killed by a boar, the symbol of winter, like Adonis, or self-castrated (like his own priests); and he bled to death at the foot of a pine tree (the pine and pine-cone being symbols of fertility).

The sacrifice of his blood renewed the fertility of the earth, and in the ritual celebration of his death and resurrection his image was fastened to the trunk of a pine tree (Compared to Crucifixion). The worship of Attis (Mithras) became very widespread and much honored, and was ultimately incorporated with the established religion at Rome somewhere about the commencement of our Era.

The following two legends (dealing with Hercules and with Krishna) have rather more of the character of the solar, and less of the vegetation myth about them. Both heroes were regarded as great benefactors of humanity; but the former more on the material plane, and the latter on the spiritual.

Hercules was, like other Sun-gods and benefactors of mankind, a great traveler. He was known in many lands, and everywhere he was invoked as savior. He was miraculously conceived from a divine Father; even in the cradle he strangled two serpents sent to destroy him. His many labors for the good of the world were ultimately epitomized into twelve, symbolized by the signs of the Zodiac.

He slew the Nemxan Lion and the Hydra (offspring of Typhon) and the Boar. He overcame the Cretan Bull, and cleaned out the Stables of Augeas; he conquered Death and, descending into Hades, brought Cerberus thence and ascended into Heaven. On all sides he was followed by the gratitude and the prayers of mortals.

As to Krishna, the Indian god, the points of agreement with the general divine career indicated above are too salient to be overlooked, and too numerous to be fully recorded. He also was born of a Virgin (Devaki) and in a Cave,[8] and his birth announced by a Star. It was sought to destroy him, and for that purpose a massacre of infants was ordered.

Everywhere he performed miracles, raising the dead, healing lepers, and the deaf and the blind, and championing the poor and oppressed. He had a beloved disciple, Arjuna, (cf. John) before whom he was transfigured.[9] His death is differently related—as being shot by an arrow, or crucified on a tree. He descended into hell; and rose again from the dead, ascending into heaven in the sight of many people. He will return at the last day to be the judge of the quick and the dead.

Such are some of the legends concerning the pagan and pre-Christian deities—only briefly sketched now, in order that we may get a better perspective of the whole subject of Pagan Origins.

What we chiefly notice so far are two points; on the one hand the general similarity of these stories with that of Jesus Christ; on the other their analogy with the yearly phenomena of Nature as illustrated by the course of the Sun in heaven and the changes of Vegetation on the earth.

The similarity of these ancient pagan legends and beliefs with Christian traditions was so great that it excited the attention and the undisguised wrath of the early Christian Church fathers. They felt no doubt about the similarity, but not knowing how to explain it fell back upon the innocent theory that the Devil—in order to confound the Christians—had, CENTURIES BEFORE, caused the pagans to adopt certain beliefs and practices! Justin Martyr for instance describes[10] the institution of the Lord's Supper as narrated in the Gospels, and then goes on to say: "Which the wicked devils have IMITATED in the mysteries of Mithras, commanding the same thing to be done. For, that bread and a cup of water are placed with certain incantations in the mystic rites of one who is being initiated you either know or can learn." Tertullian also says[11] that "the devil by the mysteries of his idols imitates even the main part of the divine mysteries."…"He baptizes his worshippers in water and makes them believe that this purifies them from their crimes."…"Mithras sets his mark on the forehead of his soldiers; he celebrates the oblation of bread; he offers an image of the resurrection, and presents at once the crown and the sword; he limits his chief priest to a single marriage; he even has his virgins and ascetics."[12]

Cortez, too, it will be remembered for complaining that the Devil had positively taught to the Mexicans the same things which God had taught to Christendom…

The issue however was that Romanized Christianity adopted the practices of these pagan religions, it was not the other way around.

Justin Martyr again, in the Dialogue with Trypho says that the Birth in the Stable was the prototype (!) of the birth of Mithras in the Cave of Zoroastrianism; and boasts that Christ was born when the Sun takes its birth in the Augean Stable,[13] coming as a second Hercules to cleanse a foul world; and St. Augustine says "we hold this (Christmas) day holy, not like the pagans because of the birth of the Sun, but because of the birth of him who made it."

There are plenty of other instances in the Early Fathers of their indignant ascription of these similarities to the work of devils; but we need not dwell over them. There is no need for us to be indignant. On the contrary we can now see that these animadversions of the Christian writers are the evidence of how and to what extent in the spread of Christianity over the world it had become fused with the Pagan cults previously existing.

Now having a slightly better grasp of the pervasive pagan influence over the early church, why is it that Christianity has been so influenced by Paganism? Is it because Christianity is just another made up pagan cult? Perish the thought! It is because, as noted earlier, the early church fathers strayed from their Jewish Roots and attempted to hold a council (Nicaea) without any input from Jewish (Messianic Jews, Essenes, Nazarenes) brothers. Had the early church fathers had any true understanding of Torah (Old Testament), they would have concluded that the pagan influences had nothing in common with the true Gospel of Jesus.

Today however, we have grown up in a faith that was built upon the foundation of mixed beliefs, those of Paganism- Romanized Christianity- and Pseudo-Judaism. The first established "Christian" (and I use that term loosely) religion was Roman Catholicism. Then, 1200 years later, came the Protestant Reformation, which lead to splinter groups forming over time such as (in no particular order) the Bohemians (Hus), Lutherans, Anglicans, Presbyterians, then we have the Methodists, AnaBaptists, Baptists, etc. and we came to the twentieth century with the Pentecostals and Charismatics. While each group has been instrumental in revealing some sort of nugget of truth which is based on scripture- all and I do mean all, are still based upon the liturgical and manmade traditions of the original Roman Catholic Church, which is built upon the very foundations of paganism.

We must get back to the book of Acts where the Church began! Jesus trained the true church elders while He was here in the flesh, then He sent His Holy Spirit to continue training them and those to come until He returns in His Kingdom. If any of these denominational groups would have simply looked to the scriptures instead of what had been done before- they would be functioning much more like the original congregation in the Book of Acts- and they would be set apart from the world instead of being intimately involved with it.

So let's begin our journey...

Chapter 2
The Origins of Easter

Contrary to what you may have been taught your entire Christian life, the story of Easter does not begin with the resurrection of Jesus Christ, but actually begins in the book of Genesis. In ancient times, there was a man called Nimrod, who was the grandson of Noah's son Ham. Ham had a son named Cush who married a woman named Semiramis. Cush and Semiramis then had a son and named him "Nimrod." After the death of his father Cush, Nimrod married his own mother and became a powerful King.[1] The Bible tells of this man, Nimrod, in Genesis 10:8-10 as follows: "And Cush begat Nimrod, he began to be a mighty one in the earth. He was a mighty hunter before the Lord: wherefore it is said, even as Nimrod the mighty hunter before the Lord. And the beginning of his kingdom was Babel, and Erech, and Accad, and Calneh, in the land of Shinar."

Nimrod became a god-man to the people and Semiramis, his wife and mother, became the powerful Queen of the Heavens of ancient Babylon. Nimrod was eventually killed by an enemy, and his body was cut into pieces and sent to the various parts of his kingdom.[2] Semiramis had all of the parts regathered after their dispersal because she had become pregnant with an illegitimate child; all but one part of Nimrod's body could not be found. That missing part was his reproductive organ.

Semiramis claimed that Nimrod could not come back to life without it and told the people of Babylon that Nimrod had ascended to the sun and was now to be called "Baal", the sun god. Queen Semiramis proclaimed that Baal would be present on earth in the form of a flame, whether candle or lamp, when used in worship, during her pregnancy she began creating what is referred to as the "Babylonian Mystery Religion"; wherein she proclaimed herself to be a goddess, immaculately conceived.[3] She taught that the moon was also a goddess that went through a 28 day cycle and ovulated when full and that she came down from the moon in a giant egg that fell into the Euphrates River. This was to have happened at the time of the first full moon after the spring equinox. Semiramis became known as "Ishtar" which is pronounced "Easter", and her moon egg became known as "Ishtar's egg"[4], otherwise known as the "Easter Egg".

Ishtar, pregnant with child, claimed that she conceived by the rays of the sun-god Baal. The son that she brought forth was named Tammuz. Tammuz was noted to be especially fond of rabbits, and they became sacred in the ancient religion, because Tammuz was believed to be the son of the sun-god, Baal. Tammuz, like his supposed father, became a great hunter. The day came when Tammuz was killed by a wild pig and Queen

Ishtar instead of telling the people of her son's death, told the people that Tammuz had now ascended to his father, Baal, and that the two of them would be with the worshippers in the sacred candle or lamp flame (Easter Candles) as Father and Son in spirit.[5] Ishtar, who was now worshipped as the "Mother of God and Queen of Heaven", continued to build her mystery religion.

The queen told the worshippers that when Tammuz was killed by the wild pig, some of his blood fell upon the stump of an evergreen tree, and the stump grew into a full tree overnight. This made the evergreen tree sacred by the blood of Tammuz. She also proclaimed a forty day period of time of sorrow each year prior to the anniversary of the death of Tammuz.[6] During this time; no meat was to be eaten (lent). Worshippers were to meditate upon the sacred mysteries of Baal and Tammuz and to mark their heads with the sign of the cross '+'[7] (Ash Wednesday); they also ate sacred cakes with the marking of a cross on the top (hot cross buns).[8]

Every year, on the first Sunday after the first full moon after the spring equinox, a celebration was made and was celebrated a gathering before the rising sun with rabbits and eggs. The festivities during this day included the sacrifices of first born children with eggs being colored in their blood then bestowed as blessed gifts and the eating of pork (ham), because Tammuz had been killed by a wild pig.[9] Needless to say, the enforced regulation of a 40 day fast from meat culminated on this Sunday with wild revelry over their ability to once again consume meat and eggs.

At this point the parallels to our modern observances of Easter should be very clear. There is a forty day fast known as lent that ends on the first Sunday after the vernal equinox, eggs are delivered by a rabbit and ham is the most popular Easter dish. The ancient Greek historian Herodotus "witnessed the Mystery religion and its rites in numerous countries and mentions how Babylon was the primeval source from which ALL systems of idolatry flowed.[10] Austen Layard said "that we have the united testimony of sacred and profane history that idolatry originated in the area of Babylonia—the most ancient of religious systems."[11]

The Bible also makes reference to these Easter idolatries:

Judges 2:11,13 "And the children of Israel did *evil* in the sight of the Lord…And they forsook the Lord, and served Baal and Ashtaroth."[12]

1 Samuel 7:3-4 "…*put away* the strange gods and Ashtaroth from among you, and prepare your hearts unto the *Lord*, and *serve him only*…Then the children of Israel *did* put away Baalim and Ashtaroth, and *served the Lord only.*"[13]

Jeremiah 7:18 "The children gather wood, and the fathers kindle the fire, and the women knead *their* dough, to make cakes to the queen of heaven, and to pour out drink offerings unto other gods, that they may provoke me to anger."[14]

Ezekiel 8:14 "Then he brought me to the door of the gate of the LORD'S house which *was* toward the north; and, behold, there sat women weeping for Tammuz."[15]

Ishtar (Easter) was also known by many other names throughout the ancient world. The names used varied according to culture, dialect and region. The Venerable Bede, (672-735 CE.) a Catholic scholar, first asserted in his book *De Ratione Temporum* that Easter was named after *Eostre*, the Great Mother Goddess of the Saxon people in Northern Europe. Similarly, the *"Teutonic dawn goddess of fertility [was] known variously as Ostare, Ostara, Ostern, Eostra, Eostre, Eostur, Eastra, Eastur, Austron and Ausos."*[16] Other names included Aphrodite from ancient Cyprus; Ashtoreth from ancient Israel; Astarté from ancient Greece; Demeter from Mycenae; Isis/Hathor from ancient Egypt; and Kali from India.[17]

Now that you have been armed with an understanding of the ancient origins of the Easter holiday and some of the remarks against its festivities from the Bible, let's now examine how the holiday began to be integrated into the Church.

Chapter 3
The Easter Revolution

You may be asking yourself "If Easter is such a bad thing, why then is it a church sanctioned holiday?" The 11th edition of Encyclopedia Britannica's "Easter" article states, "There is no indication of the observance of the Easter festival in the New Testament, or in the writings of the apostolic church Fathers." The ecclesiastical historian, Socrates is quoted in the same article as he points out that neither the Lord nor His apostles enjoined the keeping of this day. He says, "The apostles had no thought of appointing festival days, but of promoting a life of blamelessness and piety". He attributes the observance of Easter by the church to the perpetuation of an old usage, "just as many other customs have been established."[1] Early Church reformers such as Calvin and Knox protested strongly against Easter because of its pagan origins. Observance of the holiday was not widely celebrated in America until well after the Civil War.[2]

Knowing that church scholars throughout the centuries have readily admitted that Easter wasn't something to be observed we continue to dig until the root of the issue is discovered. This root reveals itself shortly before the advent of the 'Holy' Roman Empire in the early fourth century.

Constantine, Roman Emperor from 306 to 337; was born in 274, at Naissus in Upper Moesia, a son of Constantius Chlorus and Helena, and was, after the death of his father at York (July 25, 306), proclaimed emperor by the legions of Gaul. He immediately took possession of Britain, Gaul, and Spain; and after a series of brilliant victories over Maxentius, ending with the bloody battle at the Milvian Bridge, just under the walls of Rome; he also became master of Italy (312). He now ruled over the 'Western Empire, as Licinius over the Eastern: but war broke out between them in 314; and in 323, after the battle of Chalcedon, in which Licinius was killed, Constantine became sole lord of the whole Roman world.[3]

Tradition tells us that he was converted to Christianity suddenly, and by a miracle. One evening during the battle with Maxentius, he saw a radiant cross appearing in the heavens, with the inscription, "By this thou shalt conquer." The tradition is first mentioned by Eusebius, in his *De Vita Constantini*, written after the emperor's death. This miracle has been defended with ingenious sophistry by Roman-Catholic historians and by Card. Dr. Newman[4] but cannot stand the test of critical examination. Constantine may have seen some sign in the sky as he was no doubt convinced of the superior claims of Christianity as the rising religion; but his conversion was a change of policy, rather than of moral character. Long after that event he killed, his son, his second wife, several of his relatives, and some of his most intimate friends.[5] In relation to Christianity he retained the office and title of *Pontifex Maximus* (pope)[6] to the last, and did not receive Catholic baptism until he felt death close upon him. He kept Pagans in the highest positions in his immediate surroundings, and forbade everything which might look like an encroachment of Christianity upon Paganism.[7]

All the while Christianity was gaining in popularity among the people of the Empire, so much so that the pagan population began to take notice of the throngs of people that stopped taking part in the sacrifices to the Emperor, holidays, and other events associated with the pagan religions.[8] Additionally, the Christian differences with the Jewish people began to be recognized and capitalized upon by the younger Christian converts and the proponents of the Christian movement within the Empire. In Constantine's second edict regarding the Christians (Milan, 313) he granted them, not only freedom to worship and the recognition of the State, but also reparation of previously incurred losses. Banished men who worked on the galleys or in the mines were recalled, confiscated estates were restored, etc. A series of edicts of 315, 316, 319, 321, and 323, completed the revolution. Christians were admitted to the offices of the State, both military and civil; the Christian clergy was exempted from all municipal burdens, as were the Pagan priests; the emancipation of Christian slaves was facilitated; Jews were forbidden to keep Christian slaves, etc. An [547] edict of 321 ordered Sunday to be celebrated by cessation of all work in public. When Constantine became master of the whole empire, all these edicts were extended to the whole realm, and the Roman world more and more assumed the aspect of a Christian state. One thing, however, puzzled and annoyed the emperor very much, the dissensions of the Christians, their perpetual squabbles about doctrines, and the fanatical hatred of the imposed religious rules of the State.[9]

While the effort of Constantine to integrate the Christian faith into society as another peaceful way to the gods was in the eyes of polytheistic Rome a great idea; it was rejected by the true followers of The Way[10], this is because they practiced a form of 'completed Judaism', one in which the Law of Moses had been fulfilled in Jesus of Nazareth the long awaited Messiah. The early Christians had continued to meet in the Synagogue wherein they were welcome; they continued to meet on the Biblical Sabbath Day (Saturday); and they continued to celebrate the Biblical Feast Days[11]; the Gentile converts to this Judeo-Christian system also learned to live according to these same standards (Acts 15).

The Romans had little concern over either Jewish or Christian practices on their own; it was their steadfast dedication to their own gods that would eventually lead to problems. The relationship of early Christianity to the Jewish faith, and the foundation of the cult deeply rooted in a people accustomed to religious intolerance actually helped it take hold initially. The Jews were accustomed to resisting political authority in order to practice their religion, and the transition to Christianity among these people helped foster the sense of Imperial resistance. To the Romans, Christians were a strange and subversive group, meeting in catacombs, sewers and dark alleys, done only for their own safety, but perpetuating the idea that the religion was odd, shameful and secretive. Rumors of sexual depravity, child sacrifice and other disturbing behavior left a stigma on the early Christians. Perhaps worst of all was the idea of cannibalism. The concept of breaking bread originating with the last supper, partaking of the blood and body of Christ, which later came to be known as Communion, was taken literally. To the Romans, where religious custom dictated following ancient practices in a literal sense, the idea of performing such a ritual as a representation was misunderstood, and the early church had to deal with many such misperceptions.[12]

However, for political reasons, unity and harmony were necessary; and in 325 the Emperor convened the first great ecumenical council at Nicaea to settle the controversy. At the Council of Nicaea, all the Churches agreed that Easter, the Christian Passover should be celebrated on the Sunday following the first full moon (14 Nisan) after the vernal equinox[13]. In addition to this enforced recognition of the resurrection, Constantine himself had established other laws, one being the infamous 'blue law'[14], Here is the text of Constantine's Sunday Law Decree: "Let all judges and townspeople and occupations of all trades rest on the Venerable Day of the Sun [Sunday]; nevertheless, let those who are situated in the rural districts freely and with full liberty attend to the cultivation of the fields, because it frequently happens that no other day may be so fitting for plowing grains or trenching vineyards, lest at the time the advantage of the moment granted by the provision of heaven be lost. Given on the Nones [seventh] of March, Crispus and Constantine being consuls, each of them, for the second time."[15] Constantine meant for these laws and the Church Council of Nicaea to unite all contending religions into one giant compromising conglomerate, Christian leaders in Rome saw it as a great victory.

Shortly following this ruling of Nicaea, Constantine issued an imperial order commanding all Christians everywhere to obey the decree of this council. Church and State had finally united, and whenever in history this has happened persecution of religious dissenters has generally followed. Eusebius, bishop of Caesarea (270-338), generally considered to be Constantine's outstanding flatterer in the church, made this remarkable statement: "All things whatsoever it was duty to do on the [Seventh day] Sabbath, these we [the church] have transferred to the Lord's Day [Sunday]."[16] From A.D. 350, onward, the persecution of Jewish-

Christians by their so called fellow Christians began; thus the peace under the reign of Constantine was short lived and riddled with controversies. Not only was the Sabbath day changed from the seventh day (Saturday) to the first day of the week (Sunday), but special holidays were enforced under the rule of Constantine in an effort to maintain the status quo.

Chapter 4
Rites of Passage

"About 200 B.C. mystery cults began to appear in Rome just as they had earlier in Greece. Most notable was the Cybele cult centered on Vatican hill ...Associated with the Cybele cult was that of her lover, Attis (the older Tammuz, Osiris, Dionysus, or Orpheus under a new name). He was a god of ever-reviving vegetation. Born of a virgin, he died and was reborn annually. The festival began as a day of blood on Black Friday and culminated after three days in a day of rejoicing over the resurrection."[1]

The ecclesiastical historian Socrates Scholasticus (b. 380) attributes the observance of Easter by the church to the perpetuation of local custom, "just as many other customs have been established", stating that neither Jesus nor his apostles enjoined the keeping of this or any other [Christian] festival.[2] The Easter festival is kept in many different ways among Western Christians. The traditional, liturgical observation of Easter, as practiced among Roman Catholics and some Lutherans and Anglicans begins with Lent and crescendos upon the night of

Holy Saturday with the Easter Vigil. This, the most important liturgy of the year, begins in total darkness with the blessing of the Easter fire, the lighting of the large Paschal candle and the chanting of the Exsultet or Easter Proclamation attributed to Saint Ambrose of Milan.[3] This part of the service climaxes with the singing of the Alleluia and the proclamation of the gospel of the resurrection. A sermon may be preached after the gospel. Then the focus moves from the lectern to the font. Anciently, Easter was considered the best time to receive baptism and this practice is alive in Roman Catholicism, as it is the time when new members are initiated into the Church; this is also a popular practice within Protestant denominations. Whether there are baptisms at this point or not, it is traditional for the congregation to renew the vows of their baptismal faith. This act is often sealed by the sprinkling of the congregation with holy water from the font or with prayers or 'rededicating' oneself within Protestant denominations.[4]

The reason baptisms are so popular this time of year is because during this annual feast in Rome, the pagan priests would rise early in the morning and attempt to impregnate the virgin followers of the sun god with the holy seed. This is what gave birth to the Easter sunrise service; after this event, the priests would continue on to sacrifice the babies born from the previous year's festival on the altar. Eggs would then be colored in the blood of the sacrificed babes and given as peace offerings and gifts bestowing a blessing from the gods and the blood would be flicked over the people from a bucket[5] of sorts as shown in the following images…

The first image is of a Dagonic priest, a follower of Dagon (dag=fish, on=sun). The most common way of depicting Dagon is described by the archaeologist Layard, *"The Head of the fish formed the mitre above that of a man, while it's scaly, fish-like tail fell as a cloak behind, leaving the human limbs and feet exposed."*[6] This imagery is common among all the variants of the Babylonian Mystery Religions throughout the nations of the world. This imagery is also congruent with modern Catholic practices as we see in the second image which represents the fish-head mitre as worn by the Pope and other Orthodox priests.

The Catholic sacrament of Confirmation is also celebrated at the Vigil. The Easter Vigil concludes with the celebration of the Eucharist and Holy Communion. Additional celebrations are usually offered on Easter Sunday itself. Some churches prefer to keep this vigil very early on the Sunday morning instead of the Saturday night to reflect the gospel account of the women coming to the tomb at dawn on the first day of the week (which is inaccurate as we'll see later).

In The Development of the Christian Doctrine, John Henry "Cardinal Newman" states *"The use of temples [church buildings], and such dedicated to particular saints, and ornamented on occasions with branches of trees [Christmas trees, holly, and wreaths]; incense, lamps, and candles; votive offerings on recovery from illness; holy water; asylums; holydays and seasons, the use of calendars, processions, blessings on the fields; sacerdotal vestments, the tonsure, the ring in marriage, turning to the East, images at a later date, the ecclesiastical chant, and the Kyrie Eleison, are all of pagan origin, and sanctified by their adoption into the Church."*

That's right; the Easter Pageants, decorations, and all other things from the pulpit to the altar, from the shape of the building to the steeple and everything in between in our current churches are of pagan origin. And while Protestant denominations often refute any association with the Catholic Church often calling its

followers "unsaved"; they too blindly accept their 'sanctification' of pagan rites as being valid. They too celebrate the same feast days as though they were appointed by Jesus himself, and they too are as deceived as those they seek to save. So be of good cheer, for the Lord has called you to learn truth and share it with others, otherwise you would not be reading this book!

The penetration of the religion of Babylon became so general and well known that Rome was called the "New Babylon."[7]

"The Church did everything it could to stamp out such 'pagan' rites, but had to capitulate and allow the rites to continue with only the name of the local deity changed to some Christian saint's name."[8]

Fat Tuesday (Mardi Gras)

Is a celebration derived from the Roman 'carne levare levamen', meaning 'take away the flesh.' Pagans believed the best way to give up 'flesh' (meat) was by filling up on it before the sundial brought on abstinence.[11] Fat Tuesday has become one of the best known Easter festivals in the United States thanks to the assistance of the Catholic Church, government of the state of Louisiana and city of New Orleans. This is the last day a participant has to sin it up and eat meats and drink tremendous amounts of alcohol before becoming a 'holy' Catholic for lent.

Ash Wednesday

At Masses and Services of worship on this day, worshippers are blessed with ashes by the celebrating priest or minister. The priest or minister marks the forehead of each participant with black ashes, in the shape of a cross (+), which the worshipper traditionally retains until washing it off after sundown. In the Roman Catholic Church, Ash Wednesday is observed by fasting, abstinence (from meat), and repentance—a day of contemplating one's transgressions[12]; a day of mourning. As previously mentioned, a cross for Tammuz was marked upon the head of those in the Babylonian cult during this mandated period of mourning for his death caused by a wild pig. The mark of the beast is also said to be placed in the right hand or forehead according to Revelation 13:16.

Lent

The word "lent" comes from the old English "lencten," which means "spring." Created by the Catholic Church around 525, under the guidance of Abbot Dionysus the Little, this period of abstinence actually originated in Babylon, as a preliminary to the annual day that honored the death of Tammuz; and later was observed in Egypt to honor Osiris, the son of Isis, who was the counterpart of Tammuz. Again, when Nimrod died, and was made the sun god, Baal. Semiramis his wife then had an illegitimate son called Tammuz, who she claimed to be the son of Nimrod. She said that he was the "promised seed of the woman," (Genesis 3:15) and demanded that both her and Tammuz be worshipped. He became symbolized by the golden calf. She became known as the "queen of heaven," and was the prototype from which all other pagan goddesses came. Her representation can be seen in the Roman Catholic Church's worship of Mary, who is called the "Mother of the Church," the "Queen of Heaven and Earth," and the "Queen of the Universe." These titles can not refer to Mary, the mother of Jesus, because nowhere in the Bible does it talk about Mary's role in such a way.[13]

According to Babylonian tradition, when Tammuz was killed, his mother wept for 40 days, so much that he came back to life. The manifestation of this was the rebirth and blooming of all vegetation in the spring, which came to symbolize his resurrection. Again, Ezekiel 8:12-14 talks about the women weeping for Tammuz and this actually refers to what became the 40-day Lenten period.

According to Johannes Cassianus, who wrote in the fifth century, "Howbeit you should know, that as long as the primitive church retained its perfection unbroken, this observance of Lent did not exist".[14]

The Hot Cross Bun

The history of the hot cross bun goes back to the Babylonian queen of heaven (Ishtar), and a reference to it is made in Jeremiah 7:18, which talks about making "cakes to the queen of heaven." The Hebrew word for "cakes" is "kavvan" and is more properly translated as "buns." At Athens, about 1500 years before Christ, these buns or sacred bread, were used in the worship of the goddess. They were called "boun." Egyptians made buns inscribed with two horns in honor of the moon goddess, and the

Greeks changed it to a cross, so it could be easily separated. The Anglo-Saxons made buns with a cross on them in honor of their goddess of light.[15]

The Sunrise Service

Ezekiel 8:16 "And he brought me into the inner court of the LORD's house, and, behold, at the door of the temple of the LORD, between the porch and the altar, were about five and twenty men, with their backs toward the temple of the LORD, and their faces toward the east; and they worshipped the sun toward the east."

As we've already discovered, the sunrise service originated within the Babylonian mystery cult and developed over time as an overtly invasive sexual invasion of naïve followers of the sun god cults. Young virgins would be impregnated as the sun rose and those that had given birth from the previous year's invasion had the fruit of their womb sacrificed on an altar at dawn on the first Sunday after the vernal equinox. The blood from the murdered babies was collected in a basin and blessed by the priest wherein the eggs of the goddess Easter were dipped and given to followers as treats, gifts and blessings.[9] On "Easter Sunday" these sun worshippers would arise, put on their best garments and await the suns rising for it was believed that the sun would 'dance in the heavens'. In turn worshippers would often break out in sporadic dance in honor of the sun.[10]

In like mind, millions of Christians dress up for Sunday morning service every week, and hundreds of thousands more join them on Easter Sunday when church attendance is known to jump. Albert Pike, the Masonic Cult Reformer wrote that all pagan religions worshipped the sun. Whether they knew it, or not, they were actually worshiping Satan, because, as an angel, he was known as Lucifer, or the "bearer of light." The Jewish Temple faced the east, so that when they worshipped God, their backs would be to the east. Most all Roman and many protestant cathedrals, especially those with stained glass have a western facing entrance so the sun will rise illuminating the sanctuary, thus embracing the mystical aspects of the sun. We still keep the first day of the week (Sunday) as our day of worship without Biblical precedent, and the majority of us still get up early on Sunday to get dressed up and go to church every week, remember, it all started in Babylon!

The Easter Eggs

Eggs were a sacred symbol of rebirth and fertility among the Babylonians, Druids, Egyptians, and other pagan cultures. Dyed eggs were used as sacred offerings during the pagan Easter season and were also used as symbols of the Goddess Easter in various cultures.[16] During the rule of Caesar Augustus, Hyginus, an Egyptian who was the librarian at the Palatine library in Rome, wrote: "An egg of a wondrous site is said to have fallen from heaven into the river Euphrates. The fishes rolled it to the bank, where the doves having settled upon it, and hatched it, and out came Venus, who afterwards was called the Syrian goddess (Ishtar)." This demonstrates the pervasive pagan origin of the Easter egg legend; though it wasn't until later that Easter was accepted as an official church holiday in 325. Pope Gregory (590-604), forbade the followers of the Catholic Church to eat eggs during Lent, so that is when they became the official treat of Easter.

The people in Poland said that the Virgin Mary dyed eggs in various colors for Jesus to play with when He was a child. The Ukrainians incorporated blue dots in the design of their eggs, which they say represent the tears of Mary. They believe she took

41

a basket of colored eggs to Pontius Pilate as a gift, in hopes of convincing him to have mercy on Jesus. As she was making them, she began crying and the tears fell on the shells, making the dots. The orthodox of Romania dyed their eggs red, because they believed Mary left a basket of eggs at the cross during the crucifixion to appease the soldiers so they would treat Jesus better. They were not accepted, and his blood dripped on them. In Russia, there is a tradition that Mary Magdalene gave an egg to the Roman emperor as a symbolic token of the resurrection of Jesus.[17]

The egg was a mystical symbol to the pagan religions of Egypt, Japan, Greece, Persia, Phoenicia, India, and Babylon. The serpent entwined round the egg, was a symbol common to the Indians, the Egyptians, and the Druids. It referred to the creation of the universe. A serpent with an egg in his mouth was a symbol of the universe containing within itself the germ of all things that the sun develops. The property possessed by the serpent, of casting its skin, and apparently renewing its youth, made it an emblem of eternity and immortality." Thus, we see an indication that the egg initially represented serpent worship, and, by extension, Satan worship.[18]

As stated previously, eggs where colored in the blood of sacrificed infants in the cult of Babylon and among the Roman priests and followers of the Persian sun god Mithras (also Baal) during the sunrise service. This observance was not specific to the Mithraic cult, but was a common practice among pagan rites throughout the ancient world.

The Easter Ham

In the Babylonian myth, Tammuz was killed by a wild pig; therefore it only makes since to eat one out of revenge. Eating pork also expressed a blatant rejection of God's laws regarding clean and unclean meats.[19]

The Easter Candle

As we discussed previously, it was Semiramis (Easter) that stated that the spirit of Nimrod (Baal) and Tammuz would be one in the fires offered up on Easter Sunday. This fire ceremony migrated into the celebrated lighting of large bonfires to commemorate the renewal of spring through Europe and a doll, said to symbolize winter, was sometimes burned, which was called "burning the Judas." This Babylonian fire ritual is still practiced within the Catholic and Protestant churches with the lighting of the Easter Vigil and Paschal Candles.

The Easter Bunny

Because Tammuz was supposed fond of rabbits, they were chosen early on as primary imagery associated with his remembrance. In actuality, it's the hare, and not the rabbit which is Easter's main character, (In America we have more bunnies!) because according to ancient tradition, the hare was a symbolic representation for the Moon, since they only came out at night to eat. Also, the Egyptian name for the hare was "Un" (which means "open"), because they are born with their eyes open, while a rabbit's are not. Legend has it, that the hare never blinks or closes it eyes. To some pagan cultures, the Moon was the "open-eyed watcher of the skies." The hare is associated of course with the goddess Easter, and was her symbol of fertility because they reproduce so quickly.

There is also a pagan tradition concerning a bird who wanted to be a rabbit, so the goddess Oestre turned the bird into a rabbit, who could still lay eggs. Every spring, during the festival dedicated to Oestre, the rabbit laid beautiful colored eggs for the goddess.[20] So they say "The Easter Rabbit lays the eggs, for which reason they are hidden in a nest or in the garden". The rabbit is a pagan symbol and has always been an emblem of sexuality.[21] This legend of course seems like a retelling of the ancient Babylonian story in the context of a later culture; this is the same thing scores of pastors do every year in an attempt to justify their denominations Easter traditions. If you still are unsure as to the rabbit being used as an icon of sexual symbolism, then I suggest you ask Hugh Heffner, the publisher of Playboy magazine why he uses a "bunny" as his main logo...

Chapter 5
The Spring Feast

Now understanding that all of the traditions, symbols and even the very name (Easter) all stem from pervasive pagan origins, how does this affect the story of the resurrection of Jesus Christ? The Bible is clear that Jesus did live, die on a Roman cross and was raised from the dead on the third day, but the traditional context in which this story is told or fashioned from the pulpit simply isn't cogent when compared with the Biblical text, or historical perspective.

To gain a proper perspective of the resurrection of Jesus we must examine the Biblical Feast days that occur in the spring of the year; Passover (Pesach), Unleavened Bread (Hag HaMatzah), and First-Fruits (Bikkurim) found in Leviticus 23.

Leviticus 23:1-14 "The LORD spoke to Moses, saying: Speak to the Israelite people and say to them: These are my fixed times, the fixed times of the LORD, which you shall proclaim as sacred occasions. On six days work may be done, but on the seventh day there shall be a Sabbath of complete rest, a sacred occasion. You shall do no work; it shall be a Sabbath of the LORD throughout your settlements. These are the set times of the LORD, the sacred occasions, which you shall celebrate each at its appointed time: In the first month on the fourteenth day of the month, at twilight, there shall be a Passover offering to the LORD, and on the fifteenth day of that month the LORD's Feast of Unleavened Bread. You shall eat unleavened bread for seven days. On the first day you shall celebrate a sacred occasion: you shall not work at your occupations. Seven days you shall make offerings by fire to the LORD. The seventh day shall be a sacred occasion: you shall not work at your occupations. The Lord spoke to Moses, saying: Speak to the Israelite people and say to them: When you enter the land that I am giving you and you reap a harvest, you shall bring the first sheaf of your harvest to the priest. He shall elevate the sheaf before the LORD for acceptance in your behalf; the priest shall elevate it on the day after the Sabbath. On the day that you elevate the sheaf, you shall offer as a burnt offering to the LORD a lamb of the first year without blemish. The meal offering with it shall be of wine, a quarter of hin. Until that very day, until you have brought the offering of your God, you shall eat no bread or parched grain or fresh ears; it is a law for all time throughout the ages in all your settlements." (Jewish Publication Society: Tanakh)

From this portion of the Hebrew Scriptures, we plainly see the three spring festivals illustrated. The first important illustration is that of the weekly Sabbath, the seventh day of the week (Saturday). We are commanded as Israelites by birth of grating-in (Rom. 11:19) to obey the fourth commandment of God to remember to keep the Sabbath holy. We then see that the Passover offering must be made at twilight, the time between daytime and nighttime as the sun goes down on the 14th day of the month and that on the following day, the 15th of the month, we are to begin a seven day fast from leaven. This is called the Feast of Unleavened Bread. On the first and last day of this fast we are to observe an additional Sabbath day, these are known as High Holy Days or High Sabbaths[1] days because they may fall on a day of the week other than Saturday.

Lastly, we arrive at the Feast of First-Fruits or Bikkurim, which is the first day after the Sabbath during the Feast of Unleavened Bread. On this day the first-fruit of the harvest was waived before the LORD for acceptance on our behalf and the offering which the LORD required was a lamb without blemish and wine- this was to be a permanent observance. Jesus of course is the Lamb of God that takes away the sins of the world (John 1:29) and He has completely fulfilled the sacrificial requirements of the spring feasts thereby becoming our perfect sacrifice once for all time (Zechariah 12:10, Psalms 22:16, Hebrews 9:28, 10:1-18).

With this understanding let's now examine how Jesus fulfilled the requirements of the spring feasts and where that leads us in regards to the celebration of His resurrection. But first, how do we know that God intended for the Biblical Feasts to demonstrate His plan for mankind? One of the clues that indicates the feasts have more significance than mere tradition and remembrance is found in Leviticus 23:4: "These are the appointed times of the Lord, holy convocations which you shall proclaim at the times appointed for them..." (KJV)

The Hebrew word "miqra^"" translated as "holy convocations" also means "rehearsal". These feasts then were also appointed times of rehearsal for events that were to occur in the future.[2]

Passover is the first of the spring feasts. All Jewish males were required to travel to Jerusalem for this dress rehearsal with God. The instructions for celebrating the Biblical Feasts can be found in Leviticus 23, Numbers 28-29 and also Deuteronomy 16. The Passover was to be a remembrance of Israel's deliverance from Egyptian slavery. This deliverance occurred during the month of Nisan, the first Hebrew month, and represented God's first encounter with his chosen people (Exodus 12:1-14, 43-48). I suggest you read the account of the Exodus from Egypt once more which includes the Passover story; as we'll only be able to cover key highlights that pertain to this text.

Every man was required to select for his household a lamb without spot or blemish. This lamb was to be selected on the tenth day of the month and the family was to observe this lamb for five days to make sure that there was no defect found in him. No fault could be found in the lamb (Ex. 12:1-6).

On the fifth day, the lamb was to be killed at the doorstep of the home and the blood caught in a basin at the foot of the doorstep. Then, the blood was sprinkled upon the sides of the door posts and the mantle thereof. Thus, the entire doorway was covered in the blood (Ex. 12:7).

This killing of the lamb was to be done at twilight (Ex. 12:6) the Hebrew day begins in the evening just after twilight, typically around six o'clock or about an hour after sunset[3]. They would then consume the lamb the same night leaving none left for daybreak the following morning (Ex. 12:10). In preparing the meal, not one bone could be broken. This instruction caused it to be roasted on a cross bar shaped spit, so that its body could be spread open.[4]

As they ate the meal, the Angel of Death passed over the land and when he saw the blood of the lamb, he would not strike that house. Thus the people that celebrated the first Passover were saved by the grace of God through the blood of the lamb. To see how this points to Jesus should be very apparent, but we'll continue because there is a great deal more. The Hebrew word for Passover is *Pacach* which means to pass or skip over with an implication of hopping.[5] In a blood covenant such as this, trampling the blood underfoot meant rejection of the covenant, thus the reason for the Angel of Death hopping over the house when the blood was encountered.

At this point in history, Gentiles were not allowed to partake of the Passover feast unless they became circumcised (Ex. 12:48), circumcision being a sign of the covenant God made with Abraham. Later, when the Temple was constructed, people would bring their lambs to the altar in Jerusalem instead of killing them at home. During this period the Temple became the central hub for the Passover festival. So, for 1500 years before Calvary, the Jewish people had been offering the sacrifice of an unblemished lamb unto God. They understood the blood covenant and that the blood of an animal could temporarily atone (cover) for their sins; but it could not take them away (Heb. 9:12-15). Now we can fully realize how Jesus fulfilled the Passover in His crucifixion...

In John 12:1 we find that Jesus came to Bethany six days before the Passover. Since Passover begins on the 14th, this means he arrived in Bethany on the ninth. John then described how Jesus entered Jerusalem on the tenth "The next day a great multitude that had come to the feast, when they heard that Jesus was coming to Jerusalem, took branches of palm trees and went out to meet Him, and cried out Hosanna! Blessed is He who comes in the name of the Lord!" (John 12:12-13). In this Jesus fulfilled the requirement of the lamb to be set aside, on the same day God commanded when the Israelites were in Egypt.

Now that Jesus had come to Jerusalem, he could be tested to see if He was without spot or blemish. The religious leaders questioned His authority (Matt. 21:23-27), tried to discredit Him and do anything else they could to accuse Him of wrong doing. Finally, on the day the lambs were to be killed, Pilate declared before the people "I find no fault in Him" (John 19:4). Not only was Jesus set aside and tested for five days, proclaimed to be without fault, but He was also crucified at the same time of day the lambs were to be offered.

During the Temple period, the Passover sacrifices were prepared at nine o'clock in the morning due to the number of sacrifices to be made. They began the killing at three o'clock to be completed by twilight around six o'clock in the evening at which time everyone was to be in their homes consuming their Passover meal (Seder). In Mark 15:25 we see that "...it was the third hour, and they crucified Him", the third hour was nine o'clock in the morning according to the Jewish reckoning of time.[6]

Mark is also careful to note that "...when the sixth hour had come, there was darkness over the whole land until the ninth hour. And at the ninth hour Jesus cried out with a loud voice, saying, 'Eloi, Eloi, lama sabachthani?', "My God, My God, why have you forsaken me?"...verse 37 "And Jesus cried out with a loud voice, and breathed His last." (Mark 15:33-34, 37)

So as they began to nail Him to the cross, which was the spit on which the lambs had been roasted by fire (Ex.12:9); darkness covered the land. It was at this same time the slaughter of the lambs began and during the three hours of trial as by fire, Jesus finally breathed His last, just before twilight. Additionally, we must note than none of his bones were broken in accordance with the instruction of God (Ex. 12:46, Num. 9:12, Ps. 34:20, John 19:36). And, in accordance with God's instructions, those present at His crucifixion requested that the bodies of those crucified be quickly taken down from the crosses before twilight, for the next day was a High Sabbath (John 19:31). Thus Jesus, the sacrificial lamb gave his all on the 14th of Nisan as the final Passover sacrifice and He was put in a tomb (consumed by the world) at twilight thereby fulfilling the Feast of Passover (1 Cor. 5:7, 1 Peter 1:18-21).

Chapter 6
Resurrection Day

Have you ever thought about why we're told Jesus was in the grace three days and nights, but Easter is celebrated as a Good Friday, Holy Saturday and Easter Sunday, morning resurrection? Good Friday to Easter does not add up to three days and three nights, it's actually only thirty-six hours! Errors like these are often cited within the Biblical texts as a way to detract from its truth, but this is not an accurate assumption, for when one studies the original languages in which the text was written, we find that the truth is the same, but the language translation is what was in error.

The Gentile "church fathers" that presided over the Council of Nicaea had strayed far from their Jewish Roots and had lost the meaning of many of their ways, celebrations and overall contexts of worship and practice. Thus, they adopted the ancient pagan methods of worship and practice as a substitute because of the prominence the "Universal Christian" religion had received under the rule of Constantine I. For example, when the Bible translators came to a passage such as John 19:31; when Jesus was crucified on the Preparation Day so that His body wouldn't remain on the Sabbath; the scholars assumed that this meant the weekly Sabbath (Saturday) and therefore He must have been crucified on a Friday. However, the Biblical text clearly defines the Sabbath as a "High Sabbath", which takes us back to Leviticus 23 where we learn there are actually several High Sabbath days.

Jesus gave the one sign that would prove that He alone was the true Messiah of Israel and that was the sign of the prophet Jonah. "For as Jonah was three days and three nights in the belly of a great fish, so will the Son of Man be three days and three nights in the belly of the earth" (Matt. 12:40). While in the belly of the earth, the tomb, Jesus was without leaven (sin) just as the people rested without sin for this period because of Sabbath restrictions. When he was placed in the tomb the High Sabbath day of the Feast of Unleavened Bread was fast approaching. During this feast you essentially fast from leaven for a period of seven days (Lev. 23:6). Jesus in the belly of the earth is symbolic of His sinless or unleavened life being consumed by all in the world.

Again, when looking the sign of Jonah (Matt. 12:40), whenever we see the conjunction "and" we make a connection between two or more things. Therefore, when Jesus stated three days and three nights, that completes three twenty-four hour cycles or 72 hours. According to Edward Reingold's work, *Calendar Book, Papers and Code,* the date on which Jesus according to calculations made utilizing astronomy, cultural context and Torah point to only one date, Wednesday, April 3, in the year 30.[1]

If this be an accurate assessment, it means that Jesus would have resurrected at twilight on Saturday April 6ᵗʰ, or the 17ᵗʰ of Nisan. Since the High Sabbaths were special days of rest, the people did not work and remained in their homes. This means that they rested on Thursday, Friday, and Saturday- this is why "Mary Magdalene went to the tomb early, while it was still dark, and saw that the stone had already been taken away from the tomb" (John 20:1). She had been cooped up in her home for three days as Jesus was cooped up in the belly of the earth- both were ready to emerge! Since Jesus was already gone when she arrived at the tomb, this could only mean that He was resurrected at sunset at the close of the weekly Sabbath and the beginning of the first day of the week, which was the Feast of First-Fruits, April 17/18. First-Fruits is the time when the first harvest of the fields were offered to the Lord, Jesus of course being the first-fruit of those to be resurrected.

Thus we put it all together:
Wednesday (Night 1, 6:00 PM — 6:00 AM)
Thursday (Day 1, 6:00 AM — 6:00 PM)
Thursday (Night 2, 6:00 PM — 6:00 AM)
Friday (Day 2, 6:00 AM — 6:00 PM)
Friday (Night 3, 6:00 PM — 6:00 AM)
Saturday (Day 3, 6:00 AM — 6:00 PM)

With this we fulfill the sign of the Prophet Jonah as given to us by Jesus Himself. From this context we see that the death, burial and resurrection of Jesus coincides with the Spring Feast Days and fulfills their meaning, for Jesus came to fulfill the Torah requirements, not do away with them (Matt. 5:17-18). Why then do we hear from pulpits around the world that Jesus '*abolished the law*'? It's because of the ignorance of the cultural context of the life of Jesus and the Bible itself. Jesus himself stated he did not come to abolish, but to fulfill the Law and the Prophets, so whose word shall we believe, the ignorant, anti-Semitic pastor or the Jewish Messiah we call Jesus?

Therefore, when we desire to celebrate the Resurrection Day, we should do so according to the Biblical guidelines which will lead us into all truth and a greater level of closeness with our Messiah.

Today, when we gather together with our families on Passover, we should celebrate by getting dressed as if we're going somewhere and then recreate the Passover meal of lamb, unleavened bread, bitter herbs, and wine. Whatever food is not consumed should be burned by fire, perhaps make a fire-pit and enjoy an evening outside together as the food burns up and discuss the coming week long fast from unleavened bread. Making unleavened bread can become a treasured family event among Gentile believers as it is to Jewish believers. Once you learn to examine what comes into your home, searching out the leaven, you'll get an idea of how God searches through us to seek out our leaven (sin). On the day after the Sabbath during the Feast of Unleavened Bread we celebrate First-Fruits (also called Feast of Harvests), wherein we may make a special offering to honor the Lord's resurrection. These of course are just some ideas on how to celebrate the Spring Feasts and take some steps toward living a more Biblically based lifestyle. Not only can it be a great deal of fun, but it's also true- there's no substitute for walking in truth over tradition!

James 1:22 "Be doers of the word and not just hearers only being deceived"

Some additional resources for celebrating the Spring Feasts:

Seven Festivals of the Messiah by Eddie Chumney
Celebrating Jesus in the Biblical Feasts by Dr. Richard Booker
Spring Feasts of the Lord DVD Series by Michael Rood
Jewish calendar from The Galilee Experience of Tiberias, Israel

Chapter 7
The Origins of Christmas

The word "Christmas" means "Mass of Christ," or, as it came to be shortened, "Christ-Mass." This term came to the modern world from the Roman Catholic Church[1]. The Mass is the Eucharistic rite centered on the concentration of bread and wine as a real, mystical reenactment of the sacrifice of Christ on the cross.[2] Thus, through this reenactment, the sacrifice of Christ is reoffered as often as the Mass is instituted.[3]

"Christmas was not among the earliest festivals of the Church...The first evidence of the feast is from Egypt."

"Pagan customs centering around the January calends [the pagan calendar] gravitated to Christmas."[4]

Origen, an early Catholic writer, said this about celebrating birthdays in the Bible:

"In the Scriptures, no one is recorded to have kept a feast or held a great banquet on his [Christ's] birthday. It is only sinners [like Pharaoh or Herod] who make great rejoicings over the day in which they were born into this world."[5]

The Christ-Mass must be attended by the faithful, under penalty of mortal sin for not doing so. At this mass, as at every other, Christ is offered by the priest in the form of a wafer, which they believe becomes the actual flesh of Christ after being blessed; this is the Catholic doctrine of Transubstantiation. The people are to worship this wafer as the living Christ for the Vatican statements on this reveal that this worship of a piece of bread remains unchanged during this season: *"There should be no doubt in anyone's mind that all the faithful ought to show to this most holy sacrament [the communion wafer] the worship which is due to the true God, as has always been the custom of the Catholic Church. Nor is it to be adored any the less because it was instituted by Christ to be eaten."*[6]

This Vatican II statement reaffirms the doctrinal statement made in 1648 at the Council of Trent.[7] The "monstrance", the device that holds the wafer is designed to look like the sun. Thus the Catholic doctrine of transubstantiation, which centers upon the wafer as the image of worship, is actually nothing more than another excuse to worship an image of the sun god.

Exodus 20:4 "Thou shalt not make unto thee any graven image, or any likeness of anything that is in heaven above, or that is in the earth beneath, or that is in the water under the earth"

Exodus 20:5 "Thou shalt not bow down thyself to them, nor serve them"

God's commandment is pretty plain- don't worship or serve any image or likeness of anything!

When in Rome, Do as the Romans

December 25th was indicated on the old Roman calendar as *Dies Natalis Invicti Solis* — the *Day of the Birth of the Unconquered Sun*. The Roman church adopted that date as the birthday of Jesus Christ, blending their ancient culture's pagan traditions with Judeo-Christian beliefs as a way of 'converting' souls to Christ. In reality, it was simply a way to maintain authority over the growing number of Christians in the Roman Empire.

December 25th was the birth date of many pagan deities such as Apollo or Dionysus among the Greeks, Hercules among the Romans, Mithras among the Persians and those Romans who had been stationed as soldiers throughout Persia and Arabia, Adonis and Attis in Syria and Phrygia, Osiris and Isis and Horus in Egypt, Baal and Astarte among the Babylonians and Carthaginians, and so forth.[8]

However, it was the date of the Roman Saturnalia, a vile celebration in honor of the Roman god, Saturn (Mithras was the Persian version of the sun god) that was officially recognized as Christ's birthday celebration rite. The festival was originally 12 days long (the 12 days of Christmas) which began on December 20/21, which is the time of the Winter Solstice and went through to the pagan new year, we know as January 1. The Winter Solstice to pagans is the birthday of the gods; thus the sun was worshipped while at its lowest point; and rebirth occurred thereafter which was signified by the sun making its way back to its original point in the sky by New Year's Day.

The *Encyclopedia Americana* makes this clear: "In the fifth century, the Western Church ordered it [Christ's birth] to be observed forever on the day of the old Roman feast of the birth of Sol Invictus [Invincible Sun- the sun god], as no certain knowledge of the day of Christ's birth existed."[9]

Christmas also has its roots within the Babylonian Mystery Religion. This may come as a stretch to some, but the nativity's primary imagery, the "Madonna and Child" is actually imagery associated with the worship of the "heavenly mother", Semiramis and her son Tammuz also known by other names around the world such as Ashtoreth and Tammuz in Phoenicia, Isis and Horus in Egypt, Aphrodite and Eros in Greece, Venus and Cupid in Rome[10] and Cybele and Attis in Phrygia.[11]

The cult of the Virgin Mary arose in the fourth century as a result of the forceful Christian triumph under Constantine I, and blossomed about 100 years later in the fifth century. The Collyridians were, according to Epiphanius in his *Panarion*, a Christian heretical sect which began in Thrace and, by the time he wrote in 375 AD, had spread to the whole of the area north of the Black Sea and also to Arabia. It was mainly a female sect whose priestesses led the worship of Mary as Queen of Heaven. Their ritual was to cover a throne with a linen cloth, place bread upon it and consecrate it to Mary, and then consume the bread as a type of communion. Additionally, followers were sprinkled with the blood of a bull, which was a type of baptism into the cult[10]. The blood of a bull was used because of the ancient connection to Baal, the divine bull, which Tammuz was known as.

Epiphanius castigated them for their presumption because God had not given Mary any rights of blessing or baptism. His protests show the Collyridian women must have been claiming these rights. The goddess began powerfully reasserting herself in the fifth century when the feminine presence was added to Christianity by the Council of Ephesus in 431 AD when the Virgin Mary was named Theotokos the Mother of God. The Emperor Zeno rededicated the temple of Rhea at Byzantium, not to the son or a saint, but to the Virgin Mary. Gradually she was to be heaped with all the titles of the goddess of old, including that of the Queen of Heaven.

When the church began to suppress the cults of the goddess, Roman worshippers turned to the cult of the Virgin [Mary] to replace Venus. Why? Because her son was hung on a pine tree, and more ancient versions of the lineage reveal that the husband and brother of Isis, Osiris, was discovered in an evergreen. This is why Jesus is often thought to have been crucified on a pine tree and also why an evergreen is utilized at Christmas time as the centerpiece of decorum.

From this time onward, graven images (carvings and drawings) of Christ on the cross began to appear, specifically on a pine cross or mounted on a pine cone. Earlier, Jesus had been shown as the Good Shepherd; an androgynous youth carrying a lamb in his arms or across his shoulders, but when the western empire fell to the Goths in 476 AD the northern tribes, who were fond of the cross as a magic symbol, gave the push needed for, Jesus to most typically be shown on a cross, thus Catholic crucifixes became increasingly common.

Once the veneration of the Virgin was accepted, the old temples and shrines devoted to goddesses were given over to churches dedicated to Mary. The church of Santa Maria Maggiore replaced the temple of Cybele on the Esquiline hill. Another church to Santa Maria replaced the temple of Tanit, a Phoenician goddess, on the Capitoline hill. Temples to Isis near the Pantheon and to Minerva (Athena) also became churches dedicated to Mary.

An edict of 754 AD from Constantinople condemns any orthodox Christian who does not:

"Confess the holy Ever-Virgin Mary, truly and properly the Mother of God, to be higher than every creature whether visible or invisible and does not with sincere faith seek her intercessions, as one having confidence in her access to our God."

On December 8, 2003 Pope John Paul II publicly prayed: *"Queen of peace, pray for us! Our gaze is directed toward you in great fear, to you do we turn with ever-more insistent faith in these times marked by many uncertainties and fears for the present and future of our planet. Together we lift our confident and sorrowful petition to you, the first fruit of humanity redeemed by Christ, finally freed from the slavery of evil and sin:*

hear the cry of the pain of victims of war and so many forms of violence that bloody the earth. Clear away the darkness of sorrow and worry, of hate and vengeance. Open up our minds and hearts to faith and forgiveness!" -Pope John Paul II

Additionally, the Popes have stated:

Pius IX, Ubi Primum, 1849: "For God has committed to Mary the treasury of all good things, in order that everyone may know that THROUGH HER are obtained every hope, every grace, and ALL SALVATION. For this is his will, that we obtain everything through Mary."

Paul VI, Christi Matri. "The Church...been accustomed to have recourse to that most ready intercessor, her Mother Mary...For as St. Irenaeus says, she 'has become the cause of salvation for the whole human race"

John Paul II, Dives in Misericordia, 1980, quoting Lumen Gentium, "In fact, by being assumed into heaven she has not laid aside the office of salvation but by the manifold intercession she continues to obtain for us the grace of eternal salvation."

John Paul II again said, "Membership in the Militia means complete dedication to the Kingdom of God and to the salvation of souls through Mary Immaculate."

Acts 4:10-12 "Neither is there salvation in any other: for there is none other name under heaven given among men, whereby we must be saved."

While this is a brief overview of origins of the Madonna and Child symbolism within the Christmas tradition, and how their integration has affected teaching within the church; however, we are far from covering all of the pagan traditions and symbols that have been integrated into this day which supposed represents Christ's birth.

Beyond the veneration of the Madonna and Child, the nativity represents the Babylonian trio of Nimrod, Great Grandson to Noah, his wife Semiramis, and their illegitimate child Tammuz. The three wise-men represent the "Three Kings" which are not found in the scripture anywhere, but are the stars of Orion's belt and not people at all[12]. These three stars were of major importance to many ancient pagan traditions because Orion is known as "The Hunter" which is a symbol of Nimrod! Again, in Genesis 10 and 11 we read of how Nimrod was the world's greatest hunter and the leader of what seemed at the time to be the entire human race. He orchestrated the planting of cities such as Babel, Asshur, Nineveh and Calah (Genesis 10:10-12). Now if you know any history you'll know that these were horrid locations known for their idolatry and pagan practices.

In Babel we know Nimrod had a Tower constructed which reached high into the heavens. This ziggurat or pyramid like structure can still be found all over the world in cities such as Rome, London, Paris, New York, and Washington D.C. in what we now call an obelisk. The obelisk represents the uncircumcised phallus of Nimrod. Remember, it was the phallus of Nimrod which could not be found by Semiramis when she collected his body parts for veneration. This symbolism may seem odd to Westerners, but the phallus is a symbol of power to those in the East. Take for instance this quote from Isser Harel, founder of Mossad, Israel's Intelligence Agency. When asked where terrorism would strike first in America he responded "New York is a symbol of your freedom and capitalism. It's likely they will strike there first at your tallest building, because it's your greatest fertility symbol, and a symbol of your power."[13]

This came true on September 11, 2001 when the tallest buildings in America fell.

When Nimrod eventually died, the Babylonian mystery religion in which he figured prominently continued on. His wife Queen Semiramis saw to that. Once he was dead, she deified him as the Sun-god. In various cultures he later became known as Baal, the Great Life Giver, Baalim, Bel, Chemosh, Molech, Saturn, Mithras, etc.

When the beloved Queen gave birth to her illegitimate son because of adulterous affair, she claimed that her son, named Tammuz, was actually Nimrod reborn. She claimed that the son was supernaturally conceived, which lead to them both being worshipped. Nimrod became the sun god and father of creation, Semiramis became the moon goddess and mother of fertility, while Tammuz took on the role as the savior of man-kind.

When Tammuz was killed by a wild pig in a hunting accident, Semiramis proclaimed that he passed to the underworld, but through the weeping of his mother he would spring forth as the vegetation each spring season. Thus, Semiramis wept 40 days each spring at the completion of which the spring harvest came forth- a supposed resurrection from the underworld.[14]

In **Ezekiel 8: 14-16** we read:

"The angel brought me to the gate of the house of the Lord and I beheld women weeping for Tammuz. Then he said to me, you shall see greater abominations. And he brought me into the inner court where about twenty five men had their back to the Temple, they faced east and worshipped the sun."

So, all religious systems and practices in the world have their foundation in the Babylonian Mystery Cults, except for Judaism which is the branch from which true Christianity sprouted. God called a man named Abram from Ur, a pagan nation which was involved in the Babylonian Mysteries. God asked Abram to follow him and make a covenant, to which Abram agreed and became known as "Abraham" which meant, "One who's crossed over" and it was his descendents that would carry the key to knowing the one true God. So, what is a Modern Christian to do? Jesus said in Luke 14:33 "So likewise, whoever of you does not forsake everything he has cannot be My disciple."

We should forsake all the traditions and practices we have that were not taught by Christ or the apostles in scripture. As it says in Jeremiah 16:19: "…we have inherited nothing but lies and pagan gods from our forefathers." Jesus has redeemed us from that empty life we have inherited from our families (1 Peter 1:18).

Mark 7:7-9 "And in vain they worship Me, Teaching as doctrines the commandments of men.' For laying aside the commandment of God, you hold the tradition of men—the washing of pitchers and cups, and many other such things you do." He said to them, "All too well you reject the commandment of God, that you may keep your tradition."

Galatians 4:9-11 "But now after you have known God, or rather are known by God, how *is it that* you turn again to the weak and beggarly elements, to which you desire again to be in bondage? You observe days and months and seasons and years. I am afraid for you, lest I have labored for you in vain."

The Galatians were Gentiles brought to Christ through the teaching of the apostle Paul; they fell back into their old pagan worship patterns after hearing the Gospel of Truth preached. We have done the same thing! We are free of the old pagan ways and requirements. It's the legalistic pagans that demand we celebrate their days, times, and years instead of God's, this is what originally led to the integration of Christianity into the Roman Empire. So many began to refute the controlling power of Rome and began to fall away from the pagan practices that the Empirical courts took notice. Those that still obey the patterns of ancient Rome are today secure in their paths, for they are already blind and deaf to the truth, but those that follow the narrow way are still considered rogues and heretics by "Cultural Christians", simply for obeying (actually doing) what God's word states.

If you wish to become a disciple of Jesus Christ or think you're a disciple but are practicing these pagan rites; repent for taking part in these practices. Turn from this season of sin and falsehood and follow the word of God only.

James 1:22 "Be you be a doer of the word and not just a hearer only; deceiving yourself."

Chapter 8
Deck the Halls

Decking the halls of our homes, places of business, churches and yards have long been traditional staples of the American Christmas celebration. While many of these decorations are done tastefully in an effort to appeal aesthetically; some are a bit more over the top with living nativities, blazing lights, thirty foot tall trees and loud music; some with Christian themes and some secular. While all these things are said to bring warmth to a cold season supposedly all about family, few, if any, understand the underlying purposes of each respective decoration and tradition.

The Christmas tree
Green trees were cut down, mounted, and then decked with offerings of food and precious gifts to the sun god. Evergreens; because of their ability to remain fresh and green all year, symbolized immortality and fertility, thus the reason they became the symbol of the sun god- they were the only thing that remained

green. Egyptian priests taught that the evergreen tree sprang from the grave of their god Osiris, who, after being murdered by another god, was resurrected through the energy in an evergreen tree. The fruit of the evergreen is of course the pine cone, which is again symbolic of evergreen tree worship and fertility.

The Bible states in Jeremiah 10: 2-4 "Do not act like the other nations, who try to read their future in the stars. Do not be afraid of their predictions, even though other nations are terrified by them. Their ways are futile and foolish. They cut down a tree, and a craftsman carves an idol. They decorate it with gold and silver and then fasten it securely with hammer and nails so it won't fall over."

According to *A Dictionary of Symbols*, by J. E. Cirlot, the Christmas tree is also a symbol in the sense of being a pyramid. "…in European folklores… [The pyramid] is symbolic of the earth in its maternal aspect. Pyramids with Christmas decorations and lights, moreover, express the twofold idea of death and immortality, both associated with the Great Mother."[1]

During the 1600's it was actually illegal to have a Christmas tree or Christmas service in the new land of America! Those on the American Frontier had just left the confines of the Roman religious system and where fresh off the heels of reformation in Europe. It wasn't until after the Civil War that Christmas and its traditions where widely practiced, this is due primarily to the influx of immigrants from the North (European nations) migrating throughout the country.

The pine cone staff is a symbol of the solar god Osiris. Osiris originated in Egypt, where he was their "Christ", who died for the good of his people, and whose mother, Isis, was worshipped as the Virgin Mother. Osiris was an Egyptian counterfeit of Jesus Christ! This clearly shows that the custom of bringing in a tree and decorating it is associated with the signs of the heathen, the winter solstice in this case, and the Lord God does not want His people learning to do these things.

Jeremiah 3:13 "Only acknowledge thine iniquity, that thou hast transgressed against the LORD thy God, and hast scattered thy ways to the strangers under every green tree, and ye have not obeyed my voice, saith the LORD."

Long before the birth of Jesus Christ evergreens were used by the pagans in their superstitious worship. In the northern regions of Europe they were brought inside under the superstitious notion that the woodland spirits and fairies would live in them during the winter and thus survive the cold. In Italy, evergreens were used to decorate in honor of Saturn. Added to this is the fact that when Israel went into apostasy they sacrificed under green trees and God punished them for it.

Ezekiel 6:13 "Then shall ye know that I *am* the LORD, when their slain *men* shall be among their idols round about their altars, upon every high hill, in all the tops of the mountains, and under every green tree, and under every thick oak, the place where they did offer sweet savour to all their idols."

Offering sweet savors to idols under a green tree sounds like putting milk and cookies and other gifts under a Christmas tree doesn't it. As mentioned previously, it's also taught that Christ was crucified on a pine tree, because all the other pagan deities where identified with a pine tree which represented fertility and eternity.

The Garland

The only place evergreen garland shows up in the Bible is of course in pagan worship.

Acts 14:12-18 "And they called Barnabas, Jupiter; and Paul, Mercury, because he was the chief speaker. Then the priest of Jupiter, which was before their city, brought oxen and garlands unto the gates, and would have done sacrifices with the people.

Which when the apostles, Barnabas and Paul, heard *of*, they rent their clothes, and ran in among the people, crying out, and saying, Sirs, why do ye these things? We also are men of like passions with you, and preach unto you that ye should turn from these vanities unto the living God, which made heaven, and earth, and the sea, and all things that are therein: Who in times past suffered all nations to walk in their own ways. Nevertheless he left not himself without witness, in that he did good, and gave us rain from heaven, and fruitful seasons, filling our hearts with food and gladness. And with these sayings scarce restrained the people, that they had not done sacrifice unto them."

The people believed that Paul and Barnabas were sent as emissaries of Saturn the sun god, so they gathered the traditional decorum required to worship their god. You should also know that the statue of Peter that is housed in St. Peter's Basilica at the Vatican is actually a statue of Saturn[2] that was brought in from the original Temple of Saturn. Millions of unknowing pilgrims come to kiss the feet of this statue every year, so much so that the feet have actually started to wear off.

The Mistletoe

Mistletoe is also related to pagan sun god worship. Balder, the Norse sun god, was supposed to be immune to all forms of destruction because of spells cast by the other gods. The only thing they missed in their incantations was mistletoe and so Loki, the evil god, contrived to have Balder killed by an arrow made of mistletoe. After the other gods brought Balder back to life, the mistletoe promised never to hurt anyone again. It became the symbol of love.[3]

They also used it to cast spells, the principal belief being that if they held it over a woman's head she was powerless to resist, and they could then have their way with her sexually. From this comes our custom of hanging it over doorways, and the tradition that if a girl is caught under the sprig of mistletoe she may be kissed and may not resist. As it all had to do with fertility and sex, the berries on the sprig made its power more potent. Mistletoe is still considered worth more if it has berries.

And if that isn't enough for you, the practice is believed to have originated with orgiastic celebrations in connection with the Celtic Midsummer Eve ceremony when the mistletoe was gathered. During that festival the men would kiss each other as a display of their homosexuality. The custom was later broadened to include both men and women. Balder is likened to Christ in art and pagan religious custom. Shakespeare's Midsummer Night's Dream is in part loosely based around the Celtic ceremonies.[4]

2 Corinthians 6:17 "Wherefore come out from among them [the heathen], and be ye separate, saith the Lord, and touch not the unclean *thing*; and I will receive you…"

The Advent Wreath

Circular wreaths of evergreen branches were a featured part of the Saturnalia festival and other deity birth rites. These were formed in the shape of the sun, and represented life which could not exist without sunlight. These wreaths were placed on inside and outside walls during the celebrations. At the time of initiation into the Dionysian mysteries, these were worn by the initiates as fertility symbols upon the head. They represented the perpetuity of existence through ongoing cycles of life, death, and rebirth. "The use of Advent wreaths is believed by authorities to be traceable to the pagan customs of decorating buildings and places of worship at the feast which took place at the same time as Christmas. The Christmas tree is from Egypt, and its origin dates from a period long anterior to the Christian era."[5]

Today, many people utilize Advent wreaths with four candles going around the wreath. This too is a perpetuation of the sun wheel and couples with pagan fertility customs as the candles represent phallic worship. Advent is from the Latin "Adventus", implicitly coupled with "Redemptoris" or "the coming of the Savior", which if you have read this far, you know does not refer to the Messiah Jesus.

The Yule Log

The Yule Log tradition comes to us from Scandinavia, where the pagan sex and fertility god Jul, or Jule (pronounced 'yule'), was honored in a twelve-day celebration in December. A large, single log (generally considered to have been a phallic/male genital idol) was kept with a fire against it for twelve days, a different sacrifice to Jul being offered in the fire on each of the twelve days. The Yule log was originally an entire tree, carefully chosen, and brought into the house with great ceremony. The butt end would be placed into the hearth while the rest of the tree stuck out into the room. The tree would be slowly fed into the fire and the entire process was carefully timed to last the entire Yule season[6].

We noted earlier how the 12 days of Christmas was derived from the original Roman Saturnalia and Babylonian Mysteries before it. Part of the old Roman Empire encompassed the northern Germanic and Celtic territories which had migrants to the Norse territories of Holland, Scandanavia, etc. After the Pilgrims left England they went to the Norse territories and remained there for about 15 years. They left due to the harsh weather conditions, but not before adopting more of the pagan Yule-tide customs. It was then that the Pilgrims returned to England to replenish their stock to head to the new world, America. That's how America came to learn about the 12 days of Christmas.

Yuletide, meaning the turning of the sun or the winter solstice, has traditionally been a time of extreme importance in Scandinavia—a time when fortunes for the coming year were determined and when the dead were thought to walk the earth.

For a long time, it was considered dangerous to sleep alone on Christmas Eve. The extended family, master and servant alike, would sleep together on a freshly spread bed of straw[7].

In France, the Yule log is still held in present use in the form of a log shaped cake called "buche de Noel." This cake has found its way into other countries, among them the USA as a "stollen" or "hot cross bun". Using logs to decorate or shape cakes after, giving yuletide greetings, and any recognition of the Twelve Days of Christmas or Twelfth night; is giving credit to this vile phallic worship of Scandinavia's past.[8] Yuletide is also observed by witches today as one of their main high days, so if you are "celebrating" you are doing so with witches.

The Norse also sacrificed a boar to their god Freyr during yuletide. It is thought that this is probably where the English tradition of serving boar's head at "Christmas" came from and our tradition of serving "Christmas Ham"; again it all traces back to the Book of Genesis to the Babylonian Mystery Religion of Semiramus and Tammuz.

Gift Giving

The Romans exchanged food, small statues of gods (we now give snowmen, Santa statues, Jesus statues, etc.), and trinkets to one another during the winter festival of Saturnalia. The church in adopting the custom, declared that it was to again be done on December 25 but in their cleverness they deceived the masses by teaching "the three wise-men brought gifts to Christ when He was born, so we do too"[9]. "The interchange of presents between friends is alike characteristic of Christmas and the Saturnalia, and must have been adopted by Christians from the pagans, as the admonition of Tertullian plainly shows.[10]"

Should we today give gifts to our friends and to those who need them? Certainly, it is well to do this all year round, but let's not copy the heathens in doing it.

Luke 6:30-35 "Give to everyone who asks you, and if anyone takes what belongs to you, do not demand it back. Do to others as you would have them do to you. "If you love those who love you, what credit is that to you? Even 'sinners' love those who love them. And if you do good to those who are good to you, what credit is that to you? Even 'sinners' do that. And if you lend to those from whom you expect repayment, what credit is that to you? Even 'sinners' lend to 'sinners,' expecting to be repaid in full. But love your enemies, do good to them, and lend to them without expecting to get anything back. Then your reward will be great, and you will be sons of the Most High, because he is kind to the ungrateful and wicked."

Our choicest gifts should be brought to Christ.

"Now when Jesus was born in Bethlehem of Judea…and when they [the magi] came into the house, they…fell down, and worshipped Him: and when they had opened their treasures, they presented unto Him gifts; gold, and frankincense, and myrrh." Matthew 2:1-11

Give Him the best you have; give Him your life. Dedicate all you have to Him, to be used in His service. Read the Bible daily and obey its commands through the enabling grace of Christ. Only then can you have genuine happiness. But let not ancient paganism select the day on which you will worship God.

"Take heed to thyself, that thou be not snared by following them…that thou enquire not after their gods, saying, how did these nations serve their gods? Even so will I do likewise? Thou shalt not do so unto the Lord thy God: for every abomination to the Eternal, which He hateth, have they done unto their gods." **Deuteronomy 12:30-31**

"In vain, do they worship Me, teaching for doctrines the commandments of men." **Matthew 15:9**

Wassailing

Wassailing is the practice of going door-to-door singing Christmas carols and requesting in return wassail (food or drink) or some other form of refreshment. In modern times it is most commonly known through reference in various traditional Christmas carols. Wassailing, however, was originally an important part of a horticultural ritual.

In England, it focused on the apple orchards. The purpose was to salute the trees in the dead of winter to insure a good crop for the coming year. The date varied across the 12 days of Christmas. If done formally, the wassail procession visited the principal orchards of the area, caroling as it went. In each orchard, major trees were selected and cider or liquor was sprinkled over their root systems. Incantations[11] such as: "Stand fast at root, bare well at top, every twig bare apple big, and every bow bare apple now." Also, "Here's to thee old apple tree, Hats full, sacks full, Great bushel baskets full, Hurrah!" Incantations such as these were recited. To frighten evil spirits away, guns were fired into the air. Before proceeding, the procession usually danced about the honored trees and then snaked its way out of the orchard. The care with which the ceremony had been executed was measured by the crop yield the following year.[12]

Christmas caroling actually developed from a spell casting ceremony!

Incanting or spell casting is a formula used in ritual recitation; a verbal charm or spell or a conventionalized utterance repeated without thought.[13] This is the same process utilized not only during the Christmas season, but in the Pentecostal utterance known as "Speaking in Tongues", but that is the subject beyond the scope of this text.[14]

Chapter 9
What about Santa Claus?

While many are aware that children should not be allowed to believe in Santa Claus some may not realize that the origins of the legend come so thoroughly from paganism and his image and likeness are counterfeits of the God of the Bible. The name 'Santa Claus' is believed to be a corruption of the Dutch 'Sant Nikolaas' (Sant-Ni-Klaus). St. Nicholas (as he was canonized by the Roman Catholic Church) was made bishop of Myra because of his reputed piety. He was believed to have venerated the Christ-child and practiced the child-like virtues of meekness and humility. Legend has it that he gave aid to the poor, always providing his gifts anonymously. In memory of his generosity mothers would hide gifts for their children and tell them they were left by St. Nicholas. Because of his alleged piety, and legends attributing 'miracles' to him which centered on children and the bestowing of fertility upon childless couples, St. Nicholas is revered by the Roman Catholic Church as the patron saint of children.[1]

The legends of St. Nicholas bear many similarities to those of the ancient Egyptian god Bes, a rotund, gnome like personage who was the patron deity of little children. Bes was the god of war, slaughter, music, dance and childbirth, but was also supposed to be the protector of homes and children[2]. Among other things, his symbols included bells and drums. Bes was usually depicted as a bearded savage-looking yet comical dwarf, shown full-face in images (highly unusual by Egyptian artistic conventions). However, many texts point to the idea that Bes was a terrible avenging deity, who was as swift to punish the wicked as he was to amuse and delight the righteous. One source claimed that Bes was Babylonian in origin.[3]

To complete the description of Santa Claus, we find that many pagan societies have worshipped a hearth god, clad in red that came down the chimney to bless those who pleased him and to curse those who didn't, such as China's Zaowang. On December 23rd, the people living in rural areas clean out or rebuild their kitchen stoves or fire places as it is believed that on this day that Zaowang will return to heaven to report on the goings-on in the household. He again returns on the 30th day of December when people stay up all night eating and celebrating, anticipating the arrival of the New Year. There are other such red-clad hearth gods worshipped in India and throughout Asia today. Taiwan's hearth god is said to return to heaven to report on the affairs of men on the 24th day of the December. This is reminiscent of the scripture regarding Israel's apostasy in these things:

Jeremiah 7:18 "The children gather wood, and the fathers kindle the fire, and the women knead *their* dough, to make cakes to the queen of heaven, and to pour out drink offerings unto other gods, that they may provoke me to anger."

Gathering wood and kindling the fires would be done after the stove or hearth was cleaned of old ash. Making cakes to the

"Queen of Heaven" is linked to the hot cross buns and stollens we find this time of year, which are again phallic symbols. Lastly, pouring out drink offerings is linked to eggnog and milk and cookies for "other gods". Leaving these offerings under the "Christmas tree" has even more significance again when we read:

Ezekiel 6:13*"...that they offered sweet savors to their idols under every green tree."

So, here again we have the fertility connection so prevalent in the "Christmas" tradition and idolatry. Added to this is another horrible fact: It would surprise many to learn that even the name 'Christ Child' has been given to this pagan deity under the name 'Kriss Kringle' (a corruption of the German 'Christ Kindl')[4]. This has to be one of the most subtle of Satan's blasphemies, yet most Christians are unaware of it." So, not only is the Egyptian god, Bes, being promoted as a saint; he is even given the name of Christ!

Additionally, Chemosh (Hebrew , pronounced [e'mo]), was the god of the Moabites (Num. 21:29; Jer. 48:7, 13, 46). The word Chemosh meant the destroyer or subduer. This deity was looked upon as the god of prosperity and is directly related to Santa Claus in a couple ways... first, this god was also known as Dagon, the fish god (though he looked like Baal) this is the same deity worshipped in Ninevah at the time of Jonah. Ninevah of course was founded by Nimrod, King of Babylon who later became Baal, the divine bull. Chemosh is the masculine name for Ashtar (Ishtar/Easter) and could therefore be construed as a husband to Easter. Chemosh was an idol forged of some sort of metal which could be heated hot enough to consume human flesh fairly quickly. It was a pot-bellied god, which is where the fire was housed (the belly). The priests of Chemosh wore the mitre just like those of Tammuz and Mithras.[5]

CHEMOSH

It was on December 25th that the Moabite child-mass began. Followers would come before this pot-bellied god, now red hot with fire, and recite a list of their desires for the next year. Upon completion of their list they would place their child in the lap of this god to be sacrificed by fire[6].

So often when people hear what I have to say about Christmas they say "Well, it's really all just for the children." The reality of what they're saying is horrific to me as they parade their children before the pot bellied, cherry red Santa in the local mall to recite their desires for Christmas Day only to place them in his lap for judgment, just as in ancient times. Those that have been judged unworthy receive a lump of coal, no doubt reminiscent of the left over's of the Chemosh fire pit. Those guilty of this idolatry will be judged in the holy fire of a living God- Jesus the Messiah!

The following list will demonstrate twenty one attributes of God that have been given to the idol we call Santa Claus.

SANTA CLAUS	JESUS CHRIST
1. Has white hair like wool	1. Revelation 1:14 - Daniel 7:9
2. Beard-curly and white	2. Isaiah 50:6 - Rev. 1:14
3. Comes from North Pole	3. Ez. 1:4; Ex.26:35 Psa.48:2
4. Omniscient-knows about all	4. Revelation 19:6
5. Ageless, eternal	5. Rev. 1:8,21:6; Hebrews 13:8
6. Makes List of Judgments	6. Rev.20:12; 14:7; 21:27; 2 Cor.5:10
7. Checks list twice	7. Dan. 8:14; Matt. 10:26, 1 Cor.5:10
8. Gifts given on basis of a list	8. Matt.25:21; Rev. 21:27; 22:14
9. Christmas rewards once yearly	9. Leviticus 23:26-32
10. Confess wrongs to Santa	10. I John 2:1, I Tim. 2:5
11. Promise to be better next year	11. John 14:15,21; 15:10; I Jn. 2:3
12. Asks children to obey parents	12. Eph. 6:1; Prov. 6:20; Col. 3:20
13. Comes on "Christ's birthday"	13. Heb. 12:2, 2 Cor. 4:18; Psa. 141:8
14. Hour of his coming a mystery	14. Luke 12:40; Mark 13:33; Matt.24:36
15. Rudolph's shining nose to guide	15. Matt. 2:2,7,9-10; Numbers 24:17
16. Calls all children to his knee	16. Matt. 19:14, Luke 18:16
17. Be good for goodness sake	17. Matt. 19:17; Col 1:29; Phil. 2:13
18. Has a twinkle in his eye	18. Rev. 1:14, 2:18
19. Swift visit to whole world in 1 day.	19. 2 Peter 3:8; Rev. 18:8, Isa. 47:9
20. Omnipresent-Found in every mall	20. Psa. 139:7-10; Eph. 4:6
21. Says "Ho,ho"	21. Zechariah 2:6

Still unsure why Santa is wrong? Allow me to be blunt; Santa is an anti-Christ image. Santa is nothing more than a devil. Just move the "N" in the word SaNta to the end and you have SataN.

These are the origins of the legend of Santa Claus. One must wonder why the Catholic Church felt the need to place a Saint (Nicholas) within the Christmas tradition when it was the supposed birth date of their savior. Now we know; it's because there was always a deity tied to the traditions that claimed the attributes of God, so the Catholic Church had to dream up a clever way to cover it up to maintain the façade of a "Christian" institution. This is something only scholars of a completely

Gentile religion would have understood, so when the traditions were taught to the masses beginning in the fourth century, things quickly took a form hold as there was no longer evidence to the contrary because the church had severed its ties to the Jewish community at the Council of Nicaea. The remaining Jewish-Christians continued on in very small number, many of them dying off in obscurity; but the Lord Himself has intervened at various points in history by interjecting certain individuals we call "Reformers" that would reveal nuggets of Biblical truth that would serve as a proverbial slap in the face to the institutional man-made hierarchy.

In one brief paragraph, the New Schaff-Herzog Encyclopedia of Religious Knowledge tells us how the Christmas holiday entered the Christian Church:

"How much the date of the festival depended upon the pagan Brumalia, following the Saturnalia, and celebrating the shortest day of the year and the 'new sun'...cannot be accurately determined. The pagan Saturnalia and Brumalia were too deeply entrenched in popular custom to be set aside by Christian influence...The pagan festival with its riot and merrymaking was so popular that Christians were glad of an excuse to continue its celebration with little change in spirit and in manner. Christian preachers of the West and the Near East protested against the unseemly frivolity with which Christ's birthday was celebrated, while Christians of Mesopotamia accused their Western brethren of idolatry and sun worship for adopting as Christian this pagan festival."[7]

Praise the Lord for allowing you to come to the knowledge of truth and praise Him for giving you the opportunity to make a change (reform) before it's too late!

Chapter 10
The Unconquered Sun

The Roman world was essentially pagan and many converts to Christianity had come to enjoy those festivities and did not want to forsake them after baptism into the Christian church. When these half-converted church members rose to leadership positions, they made policy changes in agreement with contemporary heathen customs. And that is how we got Christmas.

"A feast was established in memory of this event [Christ's birth] in the fourth century. In the fifth century the Western Church ordered it to be celebrated forever on the day of the old Roman feast of the birth of Sol, as no certain knowledge of the day of Christ's birth existed."[1]

If the Bible contained revealed knowledge of the day when Christ was born, then we should not select a definite day on which to worship Him. Sol means "sun" in Latin, and was another name for Mithras, the sun god who was worshipped among Roman soldiers that had been posted throughout Arabia and Persia. Among those soldiers was Emperor Constantine, who had actually moved the Roman capital from Rome to Constantinople (Istanbul, Turkey). A strong controversy arose in the Christian church over this latest apostasy by Western church leaders because certain Christian Romans, as early as 354, celebrated on December 25th the Mithraic feast or birthday of the unconquered sun. The Syrians and Armenians accused the Romans of sun worship and idolatry.[2]

The planetary week wherein each day is named after a different entity in the sky, played a very important part in the worship of the sun. By the time of Christ, sun worship was most powerfully represented in Mithraism. Mithras was originally an ancient god of Iran, and had been worshipped as the god of strength and war by the descendants of the Persians. But by the first century A.D., he had been transformed, oddly enough, into the leading sun god, and the foremost pagan god of any kind, of the western civilized world. The Romans often called him by a new name, Sol invictus, "the Invincible Sun." During the early centuries of the Christian era, Mithras was the greatest pagan rival of Christianity.

And this was not without a carefully developed plan; for Satan had arranged that this religion would closely approximate in several ways the only truth in the world, that there was but one God, worshipped by Abraham, Isaac and Jacob and He begat a son called Yeshua (Jesus) of Nazareth. It had such features as a dying, rising savior, special religious suppers, a special holy day out of the weekly seven—the Sun Day, initial baptism of its converts (in the blood of a slaughtered bull), and other similarities. It counterfeited the religion of the true God more cleverly than any other religion up to that time in history.

Gradually, large numbers of non-Christians began observing Sunday as a holy day in honor of Mithras. He was especially liked by the Roman soldiers, for his worship included athletic feats of skill and "warlike manliness"[3]. Gradually, the worship of the Invincible Sun became more popular and wide spread among the Roman Empire. Emperor Aurelian (270-275 A.D.), whose mother was a priestess of the Sun, made this solar cult the official religion of the empire. His biographer, Flavius Vopiscus, says that the priests of the Temple of the Sun at Rome were called pontiffs. They were priests of their dying-rising savior Mithras, and vicegerents in religious matters next to him.[4] (Sounds like the Vatican today right? That's because it is!)

By this time, the middle of the second century, worldly Christians, apparently from the records in Alexandria and Rome more than anywhere else, in order to be better accepted by their pagan neighbors, began keeping Sunday with the rest of the empire, and in order to excuse their practice, since it was not Scriptural, they called it "the Lord's Day." Sun worship continued to be the official religion of the empire until Constantine I defeated Licinius in 323, after which it was replaced by Romanized Christianity which is simply a blending of the Mithraic and Babylonian Mystery religions utilizing the Jewish and Christian Scriptures. The reason the scriptures of these two groups were chosen is because they were the two groups most commonly causing distress in the Roman Empire.

More arguments erupted due to differences in doctrine that at any other time in history. And, because the Mithraic priesthood did not have a written codex or tradition, only an oral tradition, it was easy to adapt the other writings since they believed their stories of the sun god shared similarities to Jesus, the son of God. By this action, the Roman Church became Universal (Catholic) in that it believed that all roads led to heaven, by way of the sun god.

This sentiment is evidenced from the Pope's very mouth: "*We are in agreement that a Jew, and this is true for believers of other religions, does not need to know or acknowledge Christ as the Son of God in order to be saved, if there are insurmountable impediments, of which he is not blameworthy, to preclude it. However, the fact that the Son of God entered history, made himself part of history, and is present as a reality in history, affects everyone.*"[4]

This was Cardinal Joseph Ratzinger, the highest appointed teacher in the Roman Catholic Church on Doctrine. He is now known as Pope Benedict XVI.

Romans 3:10-12 "As it is written: "There is no one righteous, not even one; there is no one who understands, no one who seeks God. All have turned away, they have together become worthless; there is no one who does good, not even one."

A few years ago, WorldNetDaily published a controversial exposé that spotlighted one of the more frequent skirmishes in our current culture war. Masterfully written by Joe Kovacs, "Christmas in America becomes battleground" reveals the pagan origins of this esteemed tradition and demonstrates why increasing numbers of "fundamentalist Christians" are realizing that one cannot "put Christ" back into something in which He never was.

C.S. Lewis, in his book *Mere Christianity*, asserts that one of Satan's most common ploys is to "send error into the world in pairs"—pairs of opposite—" and then he encourages us to spend a lot of time thinking "Which is the worst?" Satan persuades us to argue over two options, or two points of view, neither one of which is true. Regardless of which side carries the argument, Satan wins the day.

In the current war over Christmas and religious symbols, Satan has pitted the secular humanists, who want to blot out Christianity and encourage almost any other form of worship, against mainstream Christians, who are fighting for the right to worship as they see fit by putting evergreen trees in schools and the right to "Keep Christ in Christmas". Atheists and agnostics are also rallied against Christ-mass bent "Christians"—for whom do we root?

The truth of the matter is that Satan is the real winner regardless of the outcome.

Jesus Christ tells us, but the hour is coming, and now is, when the true worshipers will worship the Father in *spirit and truth*; for the Father is seeking such to worship Him. God is Spirit, and those who worship Him must worship in *spirit and in truth* (John 4:23-24); therefore if we worship Christ in anything less than truth it could be said that we do not worship Him at all- for how could we, not knowing the truth of who He is?

Chapter 11
The True Birthday of Jesus

By now you can probably guess that Jesus was not born on December 25th as all the other solar deities have been. First, we must come to agree that Jesus always has been (John 1:1-2) once we understand that, then we can begin to look for the season in which Jesus came to dwell among man. To begin this study, let's begin in the book of Daniel. When we think of the book of Daniel we think of a boy being thrown into the lion's den; but did you know that Daniel was actually around 80 years old when he was thrown in the lion's den? He had been a ruler of Babylon under Nebuchadnezzar, Belshazzar, Darius, the latter of which was tricked into having his vice-president (Daniel) executed.[1]

When Daniel and Jewish companions (named: Azriyah, Haniniyah, and Misha'el) were younger they were taken away as slaves into Babylon and were given Babylonian names: Belteshazzar, Shadrack, Meshech, and Abed-nego and they were trained for service in the king's court and made eunuchs (Dan.

1:1-7). Daniel interpreted one of the king's dreams and was promoted to the equivalent of prime minister of Babylon which made him wealthy. The Bible also declares he was twice multiplied in wealth under the reigns of kings Belshazzar and Darius the Mede and that he was appointed as oversee of the Magi or Chaldeans, a group of astronomers and intellectuals, many of whom were also Jewish captives.[2]

Did you ever wonder why Persian (Iranian) astronomers were looking for a Jewish Messiah? It doesn't make sense until you put it in its Biblical context! Daniel had many other dreams and visions over his life regarding various kingdoms that would rise and fall, but towards the end of his life he was visited by the angel Gabriel. Gabriel gave Daniel specific information regarding the coming of the Messiah and instructed him to "seal up" some of this information. Thus, he shared what he received with his fellow Magi, instructing them to look for the sign of the Jewish Messiah at a certain time.[3]

Then we find that Daniel dies a eunuch in Babylon without an heir...so what happened to his vast fortune? With a fortune so large there would have been some sort of account for it, it certainly wouldn't have been left for the state. After the Jewish captivity ended in Babylon, many Jews stayed behind because they had attained a certain level of distinction. One such person is Mordechai and his niece Esther. So surely Daniel would have delegated the reasonability of his will to trusted companions, such as the Jews that remained behind in Babylon. Now, jumping ahead roughly five hundred years we see the treasure of Daniel reappear in the Scriptures![4]

We find that the magi have seen the sign of the Messiah in the sky above. Could it be that the same group, once trained by the prophet Daniel to look for signs in the heavens, have come to see the Messiah? For what reason would they seek Him? We'll find out in a moment...

Ask anyone you meet "How many wise men came to present gifts to Jesus, where did they find Him and how was He dressed?" As you may know, the common answer will be "Three wise men found Jesus lying in swaddling clothes in a manger." That however is not what the scriptures teach! We actually read in the King James Version in Matthew 2:11 that an undesignated number of wise men (magi) came to the house where they found the young child, Jesus, living with His mother Mary. In the Gospels we find that only the shepherds arrived at the manger (Luke 2:8-20).[5]

It's really absurd to suggest that a group of three men traveled in the middle of winter through the desert without an armed caravan. Wise men they would not have been if that was the case... The magi where in fact Chaldeans (Magi), astronomers from the east; those of the line trained by the Prophet Daniel. The same entrusted with Daniel's treasure. Following Daniels instruction, the astronomers watched the skies for 500 years awaiting the Great Sign in the heavens that finally occurred on Tishri 1, and the end of the fourth millennium (Revelation 12:1-5). The constellation Bethula (Hebrew), the Virgin (Virgo [Latin]) was clothed with the setting sun at the time that the first sliver of the new moon appeared beneath her feet. In the twelve stars above her head, the planet Ha Tzadek (The Righteous [Jupiter, pagan]) came into conjunction with the star Ha Maleck (The King [Regulus, Latin]) that is between the feet of the constellation of Ariel (Hebrew [Leo, Latin]), the Lion of Judah.[6]

On the first day of the month of Tishri (September/October), on Yom Teruah, the Feast of Trumpets, this one-time celestial alignment announced the coming birth of the Maleck-Tzadeck or Melchizadek, the King of Righteousness of the Tribe of Judah, who of course is Jesus the Messiah (Hebrews 7:11-26). During this feast the trumpets (shofars) are sounded signaling the coming of the Messiah, thus the astronomers (magi) left for Jerusalem. During their journey the Messiah arrived the fifteenth day of the seventh month on the Biblical Calendar (Tishri 15) on the first day of the Feast of Tabernacles.[7] How do we know this?

According to the Torah men were required to live in a "sukkah" or "tabernacle" for seven days, while women were free to live in the home. However, because a census has been called many men had to travel back to their homelands to be counted, so there was an unusual amount of travel away from Jerusalem. As we read in the Gospels, Mary couldn't stay in the inn because it was booked up, no room, so she had to stay in a Sukkah (Manger/Stall is a Latin/Greek description) with Joseph[8]. She gave birth in the sukkah and at this moment "the word was made flesh and sukkoted (or tabernacled) among us." In the King James Version, tabernacled was translated as "dwelt" among us (John 1:14)."

40 days after the birth of Jesus, the law required an offering to be made. So, Mary and Joseph went to the temple, but were so poor they could only afford the minimal offering of two pigeons. So, they were obviously not yet in possession of the gold, frankincense, and myrrh as recorded in Luke 2:22-24.

A time later, actually about 500 years after Daniel passed, the executors of his will have brought Daniels treasure laden caravan to the gates of Jerusalem with the proclamation, "We have come to worship Him who is born King of the Jews." Herod sent them to the neighboring village of Bethlehem, where the prophet Micah said the Messiah would be born (Micah 5:2). However, before Herod sent the magi to Bethlehem, he took private counsel with them asking them for specific information concerning the location of the Messiah.[9]

After the magi delivered Daniel's treasure to the Messiah, they were warned in a vision to secretly depart from Israel. Herod became angry that the magi ignored his request, so he ordered all male children throughout the country of Bethlehem "two years old and under according to the time which he had diligently inquired of these wise men" (Matthew 2:16). But by this time, Joseph and Mary with the young Jesus where well on their way to Egypt a trip they could not have made unless the Lord set up their flight beforehand[10] (Revelation 12:1-5)! The truth is always so much more awesome than the tradition!

So, this brings us into the Fall Feasts Days of the Bible. There are seven Biblical Feasts described in Leviticus 23, we have already discussed the three spring feasts which Jesus has fulfilled. In the summer there is another feast called Pentecost, which Jesus also fulfilled by sending the Holy Spirit (Acts 2), this holiday was originally established to commemorate the giving of the Ten Commandments on Mt. Sinai, when the fire fell on the mountain on stone tablets- the New Testament fulfillment of this is in accordance with the Prophet Jeremiah when he stated that in the last days God would write his laws on tablets of flesh- thus tablets of fire (urim and thummim) appeared upon the heads of 120 in an upper room in Jerusalem and all of them began to speak forth the oracles of God as the Spirit gave them utterance.[11]

The final three feasts occur in the fall and are known as the Feast of Trumpets (Rosh Hashanah), The Day of Atonement (Yom Kippur), and the Feast of Tabernacles (Sukkot).[12] While Jesus fulfilled the fall feasts, it was done so only in part. When Jesus came to walk the earth he did so as Messiah bin Joseph, the suffering servant; when He returns He shall do so as Messiah bin David, the King.[13]

The Feast of Trumpets

On the first of Tishri in the autumn the Jewish New Year called Rosh Hashanah is celebrated by the blowing of the ram's horn also known as a shofar. The trumpets are sounded throughout the day with the final blasts being the "Tekiah Gedolah", "Awakening Blast" which is the last trump.[14] It is a preparation day (warning) for Yom Kippur, the Day of Atonement revealing the beginning of the Days of Awe or final ten days before the Day of Atonement. This feast holds prophetic significance in that we await the return of the Messiah Jesus. In 1 Thessalonians 4:16 we read that "The Lord himself shall descend from heaven with a shout and with the voice of the archangel and the shofar of God and the dead in Christ will rise first, then we which remain shall be caught up together with them in the clouds..." We also read in 1 Corinthians 15 that we shall be changed in a moment at the resurrection, at the last shofar, in the twinkling of an eye.[15]

Therefore, this is a day to celebrate the Biblical New Year with the blowing of the shofar with a holy expectation of the return of Jesus!

The Day of Atonement

Yom Kippur is the holiest day of the Jewish year for it is the day on which atonement was made for the entire nation (Lev. 16). On this day the High Priest entered the Holy of Holies with the sacrificial blood to atone for the people's sins. Also significant is the theme of the scapegoat, the goat on which the High Priest would lay his hands and transfer the sins of the people. This is the only day the Torah specifies as a day of fasting in repentance of sin. Yeshua (Jesus) has fulfilled this feast by becoming our High Priest, our scapegoat and our atonement! It is a celebration of the meaning of Yeshua's fulfilling the Biblical meaning of Priest and Sacrifice, a day of fasting and prayer for Israel, and a day to examine ourselves and turn from sin (1 Cor. 11:28, 1 John 1:8-9).[16]

The Feast of Tabernacles

If you're going to celebrate the earthly birthday of Jesus, this is the time to do so and in a way God desires. As we've already discussed, the evidence points to this feast as the actual birth period of Jesus as a fleshly man. It is during this eight day festival that the people of Israel dwelling in tents (booths) to recall their wilderness wanderings where they had little in the way of possessions, permanent dwellings and natural provision for food. God supernaturally provided, and when they had almost nothing, God provided again! Security was not to be found in wealth of possession and we, as Israel of old, must understand that these things do not come from our own strength as people of the covenant (Duet. 8-10).

Hospitality, sharing and the celebration of the last harvest are central themes of this feast. The first and eighth days are days for assembly (Church). It was during the last day of this Feast when Jesus said "If anyone thirsts let him come to me and drink. He who believes in me as the Scripture has said, out of his heart shall flow rivers of living water. Now he said this about the Spirit... (John 7:37-39); we know from the description of Sukkot in the Talmud that this was the day on which waters of libation took place.[17]

Also during this Feast there was dancing, songs and music that took place. On the final day of the Feast there was a magnificent fire lighting ceremony in the Court of Women.[18] The Temple was ablaze with glorious light- this in all probability was the context of Jesus' statement in John 8: 12 "I am the light of the world". In preparing to celebrate this holiday, we are to build a tent to dwell in for the duration of the Feast. The tent or sukkah was built as a three sided dwelling with an open front which would welcome visitors and the presence of God. The roof was loosely thatched so that the sky could be seen through it, so while you lay you can look up into the heavens. While this is easily done in Jerusalem in the fall, when the climate is still warm, it may be more of a challenge in cooler climates. Where I live in Kentucky the average fall temperature remains in the mid 60's to mid 70's during the day but the evening can drop to the mid 40's or cooler in October. While this may be cold for some, I've grown accustom to it and prepare accordingly with some extra blankets and a tarp to stay out of the cold rain.

The point being, if you make an effort to honor God, He will honor you. So build your Sukkah (tent) and try to spend as much time in as is practical for your area; using all natural building materials (no 2x4's or nails). Decorate your Sukkah with seasonal vegetation and lighting and enjoy the celebration of Jesus' dwelling among man in the flesh. The prophetic significance of this feast is that this is the only feast mentioned to be an eternal festivity! God will someday be the sole provider for the entire earth and this feast will be universally observed for all nations must send representatives to Jerusalem to observe the feast with Israel (Zech. 14:16-17, Rev. 21:2-3).

The Lord has placed in the Scriptures the ways in which He desires to be worshipped and none of those are in accordance with the traditionally celebrated Christian Holidays. Jesus stated in Mark 4:10-12 that His disciples had been given the secrets of the Kingdom and that other people would see but not perceive and hear but not understand; Jesus taught in parables so only those that truly sought to worship Him would be able to do so (2 Tim. 2:15). For the last 1800+ years, there have been a relative few that have sought to truly make Him known, but there are billions that claim to know Him. These are the same that will say at the Day of Judgment "Lord, Lord, have we not prophesied in your name, have we not performed many good works? And the Lord shall say: Depart from me you workers of lawlessness, I never knew you" (Matt. 7:23).

My friend, allow me to be frank- if you keep accepting man's traditions and teaching as "gospel", then you will have no place in God's Kingdom. Prayer can't save you, Church can't save you,

Baptism can't save you- it's only the blood of Jesus that can save you- remember even the demons believe and shake in fear (James 5), so belief is not enough- we must ACT on what we believe and what we understand the moment we come to understand it (James 2:15-20, Titus 1:16).

Now that we've come to understand the origins of the major holidays of Easter and Christmas and the Biblical alternatives to such holidays, we'll now examine the minor holidays on the Christian calendar.

Chapter 12
Halloween

According to the Encyclopedia Britannica, in ancient Britain and Ireland, the Celtic Festival of Samhain was observed on October 31, at the end of summer. The souls of the dead were supposed to revisit their homes on this day and the autumnal festival acquired sinister significance, with ghosts, witches, goblins, black cats, fairies and demons of all kinds said to be roaming about. It was the time to placate the supernatural powers controlling the processes of nature. In addition, Halloween was thought to be the most favorable time for divinations concerning marriage, luck, health, and death. It was the only day on which the help of the devil was invoked for such purposes.[1]

The holiday was not widely observed until the twentieth century. Initially, it was practiced only in small Irish Catholic settlements, that is, until thousands of Irish immigrants migrated to America during the great potato famine and brought their customs with them.[2] Halloween traditions often involve fruit centerpieces, apples, and nuts. Three of the sacred fruits of the Celts were acorns, apples, and nuts, especially the hazelnut, considered a god, and the acorn, sacred from its association to the oak. Fruits, apples and nuts are also related to the Roman harvest feast of Pomona, who was the goddess of fruit. For example, in ancient Rome, cider was drawn and the Romans bobbed for apples, which was part of a divination ceremony that supposedly helped a person discover their future marriage partner.[3]

The combined celebration of the Celtic tradition and Roman intervention led to the festival of "All Saints", also sometimes known as "All Hallows," or "Hallowmas" ("hallow" meaning "holy," and "mas" meaning "Mass"), which is a feast celebrated in their honor. All Saints was also a Christian formula for invoking all the faithful saints and martyrs, known or unknown which is tied into ancestral and relic worship of far Eastern religions and old Roman Catholic tradition.[4] The celebration spread and was universally changed to November 1 by Pope Gregory III (731—741). He designated November 1 as the official date of the anniversary of the consecration of a chapel in St. Peter's for the relics "of the holy apostles and of all saints, martyrs and confessors, all of the just made perfect who are at rest throughout the world". By the time of the reign of Charlemagne, the November festival of All Saints was widely celebrated. November 1 was decreed a day of obligation by the Frankish king Louis the Pious in 835 "at the instance of Pope Gregory IV and with the assent of all the bishops."[5]

In some types of neo-paganism, particularly those influenced by Wicca, Samhain is one of the eight solar holidays or witches sabbats. It is celebrated in the northern hemisphere on October 31 or November 1 and in the southern hemisphere on May 1. The holiday, with Beltane (Spring Break), is one of the most popular among Neopagans, and public Samhain rituals invariably attract large gatherings. It is the last of the harvest festivals (after Lammas and Mabon); in some traditions it symbolizes the death of the old god. Among the sabbats, it is preceded by Mabon (Witches Thanksgiving) and followed by Yule (Christmas). From an astrological perspective, the setting of Pleiades, the winter stars, heralds the supremacy of night over day and the start of the dark half of the year that is ruled by the realms of the moon.[6]

Trick or Treating

The earliest mention of the term "trick-or-treating" shows up in 1939, although the practice of dressing up in costumes and begging door to door for treats on holidays goes back to the middle ages. Trick-or-treating comes from the late medieval practice of "souling," when poor folk would go door to door, receiving food in return for prayers for the dead on All Souls Day.[8] It originated in the British Isles, and is still popular in Ireland, and in some parts of England and Scotland. In Scotland and the North of England, it is called *guising* because of the disguise or costume worn by the children.[9] The ancient Celtic peoples of the British Isles believed that from sundown to sunup of the holiday of Samhain (later All Hallows Eve and Halloween) the mortal world and the spiritual world were closer and easier to travel between than at any other time of the year. This was the time that people who had died could most easily visit the mortal world. Samhain was not designed as a scary holiday until the priests trying to Christianize the benighted pagans decided "if you can't beat 'em, join 'em!" and slowly convinced the majority of people that returning spirits were bad, and that they should not be welcomed, but scared away instead. This attitude allowed the people to retain their favorite holiday traditions (putting out food for the returning spirits, parading around with candleholders made of hollowed-out gourds, building bonfires and other activities depending on the region) while staying on the good side of the church.[10]

The wearing of costumes was developed to fool the dead spirits that supposedly came back on this day. With the Christianization of the day it became even more important to dress up to fool the bad spirits- simply to continue in your traditions. In 19th-century Scotland and Ireland the reason for wearing such fearsome costumes was the belief that since the spirits that were abroad this night were essentially intent on doing them harm, the best way to avoid this was to fool the spirits into believing that you were one of them.[11]

Symbolism

While Halloween can be identified by anything from the Devil and Ghosts to Frankenstein and Dracula its primary image is that of the Jack- o- lantern. A jack-o'-lantern is a pumpkin, turnip or rutabaga whose top and stem have been carved off and interior removed to leave a hollow shell. Sections of a side are carved out to make a design, usually a face and then a light source (typically a candle) is inserted in hollowed shell to illuminate the face. This practice began in Ireland and is practiced throughout Europe primarily by carving the readily available beet, turnip, or rutabaga. The Pumpkin which was more readily available in the America's is the most popular today.[12]

The practice of carving a jack-o'-lantern goes back to the Irish legend of Jack, a lazy but shrewd farmer who used a cross to trick the Devil, then refused to free him unless he agreed to never let Jack into Hell. The Devil agreed. When Jack died, he was too sinful to be allowed into Heaven, but the Devil wouldn't let him into Hell. So, Jack carved out one of his turnips, put a candle inside it, and began endlessly wandering the Earth for a resting place. He was known as "Jack of the Lantern", or Jack-o'-Lantern.[13]

There are variations on the legend. Some of which include:

The Devil mockingly tossing a coal from the fires of Hell at Jack, which Jack then places in the turnip.

Jack tricking/trapping the Devil a variety of ways, including placing a key or other item in the Devil's pocket when the Devil is suspended in the air or plucking an apple from a tree.

Jack's bargain with the Devil being different. In some variations, the deal is only a temporary bargain, but the Devil, embarrassed and vengeful, refuses Jack entry after Jack dies.

The Catholic Church tells the tale of Jack as an independent man who out smarted the devil trying to make his own way to heaven, but fell short. His spirit is celebrated in the commemoration of the Jack o Lantern.[14]

While the Catholic Church readily denounces the practices of astrology, palm reading, etc. as shown below:

"All forms of divination are to be rejected: recourse to Satan or demons, conjuring up the dead or other practices falsely supposed to "unveil" the future. Consulting horoscopes, astrology, palm reading, interpretation of omens and lots, the phenomena of clairvoyance, and recourse to mediums all conceal a desire for power over time, history, and, in the last analysis, other human beings, as well as a wish to conciliate hidden powers.

They contradict the honor, respect, and loving fear that we owe to God alone."[15]

However, they (Catholic Church) implement other forms of divination and necromancy in their holidays and mass celebrations. We of the protestant faiths such as Methodists, Baptists, Pentecostals, etc. often fail to understand that while we protested against some aspects of the Roman Catholic Church- much of their teachings remained in our interpretation of religion, especially when looking at denominational liturgy and holiday celebration. Denominations still practicing these things while renouncing other Roman doctrines are still to be considered the daughters of Babylon. The only way out is to simply flea and find a group that teaches and practices pure Biblical truth in a vein like that of the 1st Century Church.

Chapter 13
St. Valentine's Day

The feast of Saint Valentine was formerly celebrated on February 14 by the Roman Catholic Church until the revised calendar 1969 which is when the feast was removed as a church feast, but by that time it had taken hold within the marketplace and had developed into a cash cow for various industries. The feast of St. Valentine was first decreed in 496 by Pope Gelasius I, who included Valentine and Saint George among those "…whose names are justly reverenced among men, but whose acts are known only to God."[1] The creation of the feast for such dimly conceived figures may have been an attempt to supersede the pagan holiday of Lupercalia that was still being celebrated in 5th century Rome, on February 15.[2]

The saint's feast day was removed from the Church calendar in 1969 as part of a broader effort to remove saints viewed by some as being of purely legendary origin, for there is no evidence pointing to St. Valentine as ever having existed.[3] The feast day is still celebrated locally in some parishes, as well as by those Catholics who follow the older, pre-Vatican II calendar.[4] Prior to this action, the church in Rome that had been dedicated to him observed his feast day by, among other things, displaying his reputed skull surrounded by roses, much like the iconography often used by the Grateful Dead.[5]

Juno Fructifier & the Lupercalia

On February 14th the festival to honor the goddess Juno Fructifier was celebrated through the exchange of cards dropped into a box anonymously. Women would drop cards in a common box and men would each draw one out. These two would be a couple for the duration of the festival and sometimes longer. The Lupercalia was an annual Roman festival, held on February 15 to honor Faunus (Pan), god of fertility and forests. The festival was celebrated near the cave of Lupercal on the Palatine (one of the seven Roman hills), to expiate and purify new life in the spring. This festival's origins are older than the founding of Rome.[6]

The religious ceremonies were directed by the *Luperci*, the "brothers of the wolf (*lupus*)" thought to be priests from the line of Romulus and Remus the founders of Rome. During Lupercalia, a dog and two male goats were sacrificed. Two patrician (elite caste in ancient Rome) youths were anointed with their blood, which was wiped off with wool soaked in milk, after which they were expected to smile and laugh. The Luperci afterwards dressed themselves in the skins of the sacrificed goats, in imitation of Lupercus, and ran round the Palatine Hill with thongs cut from the skins fashioned into whips called Februa. Girls and young women would line up on their route to receive lashes from these whips. This was supposed to ensure fertility and ease the pains of childbirth. This tradition itself has survived (christened and shifted to spring) in certain Easter Monday ritual whippings.[7]

The feast of St. Valentine was first declared to be on February 14 by Pope Gelasius I in 496. He created the day to counter the practice held on Lupercalia of young men and women pairing off as lovers by drawing their names out of an urn, but this practice is not attested in any sources from that era. This was another failed attempt to Christianize the pagans of Rome. Now that we know that Valentine's Day was created to Christianize the Lupercalia[8]; let's look at the symbols associated with it.

Cupid

In Greek and Roman mythology, Cupid is the god of erotic love. He is equated with the Greek god Eros and one of his Latin names is Eros (from which we get erotic). He is also called Amor, Latin for love. He was the spawn of Aphrodite and Ares[9] (Semiramus and Nimrod) which would make him an incarnation of Tammuz. In painting and sculpture, Cupid is portrayed as a nude winged boy armed with a bow and a quiver of arrows. The traditional Christian depiction of a cherub is based on him and not Biblical description. On gems and other surviving pieces of art, he is usually shown amusing himself with childhood play, sometimes driving a hoop, throwing darts, catching a butterfly, or flirting with a nymph. He is often depicted with his mother (in graphic arts, this is nearly always Venus), playing a horn.[10]

Pan

The parentage of Pan (Faunus) is unclear; in some legends he is the son of Zeus and in some he is the son of Hermes. His mother is said to be a nymph; whatever the case, it surely leads us back to the Babylonian Mystery Religion. His nature and name is alluring, particularly since often his name is mistakenly thought to be identical to the Greek word pan, meaning "all", when in fact the name of the god is derived from the word "paon", which means "herdsman" and shares its prefix with the modern English word "pasture".[11]

Apparently when Pan was a newborn, the first onlookers saw the ugly "child" and ran in fright (or panic) which is what led him to wander the woodlands. Of course, Pan was later known for his musical flute, capable of arousing inspiration, sexuality, or panic, depending on his intentions.[12] Pan is one of the prototype deities invoked in the neo-pagan archetype of the "horned god" (Molech); this is also evidenced in cultic groups such as the Bohemian Club to which many well known politicians and business men belong[13]. Pan is famous for his sexual prowess, and is often depicted with an erect phallus. He was believed by the Greeks to have plied his charms primarily on maidens and shepherds.

It is likely that the demonized images of the incubus and even the horns and cloven hooves of Satan, as depicted in much Christian literature and art, were taken from the images of the highly sexual Pan.[14] This is the same creature featured in the Walt Disney film "The Chronicles of Narnia" and C.S. Lewis book by the same title as "Mr. Tumnus".

Valentine's Cards

Each year millions of school aged children trade Valentine's Cards and again, this too originated within the Roman festival on February 14th to honor Juno Fructifier, Queen of the Roman gods and goddesses as well as goddess of marriage. In one ritual, women would submit their names to a common box and men would each draw one out. These two would be a couple for the duration of the festival (and at times for the entire following year). Both rituals were designed to promote not only fertility, but also life generally.[15]

The giving of other gifts such as chocolates, roses, diamonds, etc. are all outcroppings of the commercialism of America and bear no significant pagan influence in of themselves. So yet again, we have another pagan holiday in honor of foreign gods to which we should have no allegiance whatsoever. So often I have heard it said "I know it's pagan, but it's all in good fun", regardless of how we try and rationalize our disobedience to God- it's the most simple form of idolatry, regardless of whether or not we understand it- God does. This is why we are admonished to study to show ourselves approved unto God (2 Tim. 2:15).

James 4:17 "Remember, it is sin to know what you ought to do and then not do it."

Chapter 14
St. Patrick's Day

Saint Patrick is the patron saint of Ireland, along with Saint Brigid, the pagan goddess of fire, and Saint Columba, missionary to Scotland.[1]Patrick's autobiographical *Confessio* at the age of about sixteen Patrick was captured and taken to Ireland as a slave to a Druidic chieftain named Milchu. Although he came from a Catholic family, he was not particularly religious before his capture. However, his enslavement markedly strengthened his faith. It was at this time he learned the native Celtic language and the customs of the druids, as his master was a druidic high priest.[2]

He escaped at the age of twenty-two as legend has it under the direction of an angel, and spent twelve years in a monastery in Auxerre, where he adopted the name Patrick (*Patricius*, in Old Irish spelled *Pádraig*). One night he heard voices begging him to return to Ireland, and he thus, by now in his thirties, became one of the first Christian missionaries in Ireland, being preceded by

Palladius. Britain at this time was undergoing turmoil following the withdrawal of Roman troops in 407 and Roman central authority by 410. Having been under the Roman cloak for over 350 years, the Romano-British had learned to look after themselves. Populations were on the move on the European continent, and the recently converted "Christian" Britain was being colonized by Anglo-Saxons.[3]

One famous story relates that at the annual vernal fire (bone fire) that was to be lit by the High King at Tara, when all the fires were extinguished so they could be renewed from the sacred fire from Tara, Patrick lit a rival fire, a miraculously inextinguishable "Christian" bonfire on the hill of Slane at the opposite end of the valley. The season was associated with the Pagan Easter (Easter Candles) by chroniclers who followed Patrick's own account in his *Confessio.*[4]

Legend also credits Patrick with teaching the Irish about the concept of the Trinity by showing people the shamrock, a three-leaved clover, using it to highlight the Christian dogma of 'three divine persons in the one God'. While Patrick was not the first missionary to Ireland, he was the most influential. Patrick is also responsible for the hindrance of Crom Cruach (Chief Pagan God of Sun and Fertility) worship in Ireland.[5] Legend has it that Patrick cursed and destroyed the lands largest idol.

Now that we have a better understanding of Saint Patrick, we must ask ourselves; "What's the problem with celebrating his missionary journey through Ireland?" Nothing is wrong with thanking God for sending someone to Ireland to preach the gospel. But where does the need for celebration come in and where does the thanking of God actually take place during this

'Holy' day? Thousands of missionaries go all over the world everyday- do we celebrate or even recognize them for it? Not at all! The majority of those truly serving the Lord do so without a title, without recognition and without institutional church sanctioning.

The Paganization of an honorable day

St. Patrick's Day was supposedly instituted to memorialize the death of Saint Patrick and it became an official Irish feast day (holy day) when Patrick was named patron saint of Ireland by the Roman Catholic Church. This all sounds fine and well; however upon further examination you'll find that in addition to the celebration of Patrick, the day came to include the celebrations of Celtic gods, political agendas, and Pagan Celtic culture.

In America most all of the St. Patrick's Day festivals are organized by the Ancient Order of Hibernians (AOH). The AOH is an Irish-Catholic fraternal organization which is known to be anti-protestant. This organization is known in Ireland as far back as 1556 when it was founded to protect Irish Catholics from the persecution of English Protestants. It had a historical concept of itself as a continuation of the 1541 rebellion, a Catholic uprising which attempted to wipe out the Protestant Plantations and to extirpate "heresy" (by which was meant Protestantism) in Ireland.[6]

As a vehicle for Irish nationalism, the AOH greatly influenced the ultra-sectarian course of Irish politics in the early twentieth century and by 1914 had saturated the entire island. When it was first founded in the United States, its existence and activities were concealed for some years. "*What where some of the 'concealed' activities of the AOH"* you ask? The introduction of Celtic-Catholic ideologies and culture of course; thus, the AOH began the facilitation of 'St. Patty's Day' parades all over the country.

You may say "Well, what's wrong with one country trying to spread its culture and national pride through parades?" You missed the point! Ireland was and still is in many respects pagan (Celtic-Catholic). So much so that the Catholic Church made the island's Pagan Priestess (Brigit) a saint right along with St. Patrick! Additionally, the Celtic pagans primarily worshipped nature spirits, but they being under Roman control at the time, also adopted many Roman gods such as Dionysius the god of beer (ale). Beer drinking is another major function at the St. Patrick's Day parades, which is simply another example of the perpetuation of pagan belief and culture through modern inventions and ignorance.

Celtic Symbolism

Would Saint Patrick approve of the festivities and revelry that take place during his 'holy day'? Better yet, would he approve of the symbolism associated with this celebration? Webster tells us that a symbol is "something that stands for or suggests something else by reason of relationship, association, convention, or accidental resemblance; esp: **a visible sign of something invisible**."[7] With this definition in mind, let's look at the visible symbolic manifestations of the invisible demonic realm by examining the leprechauns, shamrocks, and four-leaf clovers.

Leprechauns

These little green men dressed in shoe makers garb hide their treasures at the ends of rainbows, so the story goes. But how did they become associated with an Irish Saint's holiday? We touched on the fact that Ireland has three "patron saints", one of which was a former pagan goddess of fire. 'Saint' Brigit as she is now known was once a Wiccan priestess; which is essentially a nature worshipper. They believe in 'Elementals' which are "creatures evolved in the four kingdoms of earth, fire, air, and water. They (elementals) are also known as gnomes, sylphs, salamanders, and undines (pixies, fairies, trolls, dwarfs, nixies, goblins, leprechauns, banshees, moss people, white ladies, wild women, men of peace, jinn, devs, dryads, elves and fauns). They may also be termed as the forces of nature, and will either operate effects as the servant agents of general devic law, or may be employed by the disembodied spirits- whether pure or impure- and by living adepts of magic and sorcery produce a desired phenomenal result. Such beings never become men."[8]

Elementals are the spirits that demons essentially "boss around" according to over 30 new age and occult texts consulted.

"These elementals are the principle agents of disembodied but never visible spirits at séances, and the producers of all phenomena except the subjective."[9] So again, a leprechaun, pixie, etc. is the manifestation of the will of a disembodied spirit. All of the elemental beings are 'light beings' which means that they can "slip into whatever form your mind imagines as a means to communicate with your spirit."[10]

A leprechaun is a nature spirit (elemental). This spirit is also on "Lucky Charms" Cereal boxes; by the way the word cereal comes from 'Ceres', the goddess of grain.[11] In the "*Seeker's Handbook*" we are told that elementals are "creatures who figure strongly in ceremonial magic and practices of nature-worship, or wicca".

There's an Irish Blessing that states:

Near a misty stream in Ireland in the hollow of a tree Live mystical, magical leprechauns who are clever as can be With their pointed ears, and turned up toes and little coats of green. The leprechauns busily make their shoes and try hard not to be seen. Only those who really believe have seen these little elves. And if we are all believers, we can surely see for ourselves.[12]

Legend has it that under the threat of physical violence, the Leprechaun will take you to his pot of gold at the end of the rainbow; but if you take your eyes off him for even a second, he'll disappear. No one knows where the pot of gold idea came from, but it's thought to be another incantation for a spirit to produce what a greedy person desires. Lastly, leprechauns and all other elementals answer to Pan the god of the nature elementals.

Again, Pan is the horned man being with a goat's lower body typically pictured as Satan. The Dictionary of Mysticism admits: [Pan also known as the Egyptian Baphomet] "Baphomet is the sabbatical goat, in whose form Satan was said to be worshipped at the witches sabbath".[13] Coincidentally, the witches sabbaths occur on all the Catholic Holy Days and none of the Biblical Feast Days!

This again is due to the fact that Emperor Constantine "Christianized" all pagan beliefs during his reign. During the middle ages, under the Church/State rule of the Roman Catholic Church, Catholics labeled Saturday as the "Witches Sabbath" and persecuted all who worshipped God and His Christ on this day.[14] This is because Jews and those of Judeo-Christian heritage refused to break the Lord's Sabbath Day (Saturday) by acknowledging the power of the church to change times and laws. The Roman Church was making war against the true saints of God. (see Daniel 7:21-25)

Pan is also associated with Peter Pan[15] believe it or not! Peter Pan is nothing more than a big leprechaun. He is the fairy overseer in Never Land, when people state their disbelief in fairies, one dies and Peter loses power. The most interesting facet about this fact is that when researching the author of Peter Pan, J.M. Barrie the Wikipedia Encyclopedia states about him: *"Although some people may find his friendship with children suspicious, there does not seem to be any evidence that anything inappropriate happened, and the youngest of the boys, Nico, flatly denied that Barrie ever behaved inappropriately; some biographers suggest that he may have been asexual. To that extent he may have been fey; his work characteristically taking us beyond the temporal, sexual, material preoccupation of contemporary Western consciousness back into another earlier world reminiscent of the Gaelic 'Tír Na nÓg', the mythic land of perpetual youth."* [16]

Tír na nÓg, called in English the Land of the Young, was the most popular of the Otherworld's in Irish mythology.[17]

The Shamrock

The shamrock (Irish *seamróg*) is a plant with trifoliate leaves and it is a symbol of St. Patrick's Day because tradition has it that St. Patrick used the plant to explain the theological doctrine of the

Holy Trinity (three persons in one God). The word is a diminutive of Irish *seamar*, "clover." The ancient Druids associated the shamrock with the coming of spring and the rebirth of the natural world at the vernal equinox (Easter). However, the four-leaf clover actually dates back to before Christianity to the Pagan period, when clovers were widely considered Celtic charms. Celtic dominance once extended across Ireland, and it was originally the Druids (otherwise known as Celtic priests) who ascertained that the clover was potent against malevolent spirits, the four leaf variety serving as a sort of talisman, thus thrusting its status as a good luck charm into mainstream society.[18]

The four-leaf clover as a talisman for luck and good fortune brings us back to our famous cereal leprechaun's slogan "They're after me Lucky Charms"[19]; notice all the marshmallows in this cereal are talismans for good luck. According to The American Heritage Dictionary of the English Language a Talisman is:

An object marked with magic signs and believed to confer on its bearer supernatural powers or protection.

Something that apparently has magic power.

In either event, the Shamrock and four-leaf clovers predate Christianity in their usage as symbols of pagan religion.

Ephesians 5:11 "And have no fellowship with the unfruitful works of darkness, but rather reprove them."

Chapter 15
New Year's Day

New Year's Day is the first day of the year in the Gregorian calendar. In modern times, it is January 1. In most countries, it is a holiday. It is a holy day to many of those who still use the Julian calendar, which includes followers of some of the Eastern Orthodox churches, and is celebrated on January 14 of the Gregorian calendar due to differences between the two calendars. This day is traditionally a religious feast, but since the 1900s, has become an occasion for celebration on the night between December 31 and January 1, called New Year's Eve. There are often fireworks at midnight.

It is also an occasion to make New Year resolutions, which they hope to fulfill in the coming Year; the most popular ones in the western world include stopping tobacco smoking or drinking, or to lose weight or get physically fit.[1]

Among the 7th century druidic pagans of Flanders and the Netherlands, it was the custom to exchange gifts at the New Year, a pagan custom deplored by Saint Eligius (Missionary to the druids of Flanders, France), who warned the Flemings and Dutchmen, "[Do not] make vetulas, [little figures of the Old Woman], little deer or iotticos or set tables [for the house-elf, see Puck] at night or exchange New Year gifts or supply superfluous drinks [another Yule custom]." The quote is from the vita of Eligius written by his companion Ouen.[2]

The ancient Roman calendar had only ten months and started the year on March 1st, which is still reflected in the names of some months which derive from Roman numerals: September (Seventh), October (Eighth), November (Ninth), December (Tenth). Around 715 BC the months of January, February and Mercedonius were added to the end of the year (Mercedonius in leap years only). Because consuls were chosen in January, and because years were named after the consuls who served in that year, January became the de facto beginning of the year. In 45 BC Julius Caesar introduced the Julian calendar, dropping Mercedonius and decreeing that the New Year should start on January 1st.[3]

He chose January because in Roman mythology Janus was the god of gates, doors, doorways, beginnings, and endings. Janus was frequently used to symbolize change and transitions such as the progression of past to future, of one condition to another, of one vision to another, the growing up of young people, and of one universe to another. Hence, Janus was worshipped at the beginnings of the harvest and planting times, as well as marriages, births and other beginnings. He was representative of the middle ground between barbarity and civilization, rural country and urban cities, and youth and adulthood. Janus of course is the root where we derive the word January.

Again; there is no Biblical president for the changing of days, times, and laws! The Bible actually warns us against doing such things: **Daniel 7:25** "And he shall speak great words against the most High, and shall wear out the saints of the most High, and think to change times and laws: and they shall be given into his hand until a time and times and the dividing of time."

The "he" in Dan. 7:25 is referring to the Beast, more commonly known as the Beast of Revelation which operate through the spirit of anti-Christ, which I believe these pagan priests and emperors where influenced by.

Symbolism

In the United States, a common image used for New Years is that of an incarnation of Father Time (or the "Old Year") wearing a sash across his chest with the previous year printed on it passing on his duties to the Baby New Year (or the "New Year"), an infant wearing a sash with the new year printed on it.[4]

Father Time

Father Time is a mythical personification of time. He is usually depicted as an elderly bearded man, dressed in a robe, carrying an hourglass or other timekeeping device (representing time's constant movement). This image is culled from several sources, including the Holly King, the Celtic god of the dying year, and Chronos, the Greek god of time.

Chronos (also known as Chronus) is the personification of time itself. Indeed, the word means "time" and is the root of "chronology" and other modern words. In Greek mythology Chronos was a Titan and not a god; he was the Titan of Time.[5]

Saturn (referred to by the Greeks as Chronos) was the Roman sun god and keeper of time. Male ruler of the Roman Gods prior to Jupiter, Saturn's weapon was a scythe or sickle. The Romans honored Saturn at a Mid-Winter festival called Saturnalia (Christmas), which lasted several days and at which there was much feasting and making merry of which January 1st was the end of the 12 day festival (12 days of Christmas).

In various New Year's Eve customs, Father Time's image is used as the personification of the previous year (or "the Old Year"), who "hands over" the duties of time to the Baby New Year (or "the New Year"). In this case, his old age is emphasized (in particular, he may be depicted walking with the aid of a stick). Sometimes, due to the relationship between death and aging, Father Time is associated with the Grim Reaper. This demonstrates yet another representation of the pagan cycles of life, death and rebirth that have been carried over into the modern Church from the ancient pagan festivals.

Therefore, while it may be of modern necessity to accept January 1st as the beginning of the year for civic reasons; it's not necessary to partake of the festivities seeing as they're the completion of the Christmas holiday and once again have their roots pervasively bound within paganism.

Ephesians 5:16-17 "Redeem the time, because the days are evil. Therefore do not be foolish but understand what the will of the Lord is."

Chapter 16
Where do we go from here?
"We must learn to love God more than our ideals of God."[1]

Many believe that it is only the Jews that are to celebrate the "Jewish Holidays" (Biblical Feast Days) and that God somehow gave all the blessings and new holidays to the Christians in place of the Jews. This replacement theology is satanic. Additionally, the Bible never states that the feast days are "Jewish"; it specifically states that they are "The Feasts of the Lord" (Lev. 23), they are literally His holidays! The issues are further resolved in the book of Acts, chapter 15 vs. 20 & 29 which states the four things Gentiles are to abstain from; 1) Pollution from or Meat sacrificed unto idols, 2) fornication, 3) blood, and 4) from things strangled. Now, while these four things seem to indicate simple eating and moral issues, upon deeper examination we'll find that the meaning is much deeper.

Fornication we should understand includes lust of the mind and heart, adultery, and sex out of wedlock. Blood, can be avoided by eating meats that are fully cooked and by not baptizing converts in the blood of bulls or infants which was a common heathen practice still practiced in modern Voodoo, Santeria, and some Pagan Festivals. So, no more rare steaks! Things strangled means not choking your food to death or eating animals killed by strangulation; we are to process food humanely. Now, we come to 'pollution from' or 'meat sacrificed unto' idols.

The word 'pollution' according to Strong's Concordance actually means 'ceremonial defilement', this means religiously acknowledging anything besides Christ in worship. "Meats offered unto" in verse 29, again according to Strong's Concordance, actually means "images sacrificed unto", this means giving an image to an unseen deity is a sacrifice unto the unseen deity. This is a powerful truth because we have given an image of a man to Jesus and we put that image on pictures, statues, crucifixes, t-shirts and everywhere else we can make a dollar or 'focus' our religious attention when the simple fact is we have ceremonially given an image sacrifice to an unseen deity whom we call our god- which makes it an idol.

So yes- a crucifix or picture of "Jesus" is an idol, which means you've broken the second commandment. And yes, putting up a Christmas tree in your home is classified as ceremonial defilement for your placing an object worshipped by Egyptian, Roman, Norse and Germanic cults in your home. The Bible is clear that "blessed are those that believe and do not see", we have nothing other than a vague description of Christ- certainly not enough for a painting or photo. Why? Because He knew in our ignorance we would worship His image over Him! And Jeremiah 10:2-4 states that the heathen would bring trees into their homes to decorate them and their devotion was in vain (self serving).

We have also ascribed image sacrifices to Ishtar by way of Mary and by way of the Easter Bunny, to the Egyptian god Bes by way of Santa Claus, and to Mithras the sun god with the Crucifix and statues of Christ and to Zeus with portraits of Christ. Thus, we are all guilty of idolatry! If we rid ourselves of idolatry we rid ourselves of all Christian Holidays! If we can do this (which we can!) we can begin to fulfill the greatest commandment, loving God with all our heart, soul, and mind (Matthew 22:37).

Jesus said to the Samaritan woman at the well in John 4:22 "You don't know what God you worship; but we Jews know what God we worship for salvation is of the Jews". The fact is, until we repent of mixing paganism with the worship of the God of Israel we are guilty of worshipping unknown gods.

Is it sin to celebrate the Christian holidays? Yes! Will you go to hell for it? The wages of sin is death (Rom 6:23) It's time to stop heaping up for yourselves teachers that tell your itching ears the things you want to hear (2 Tim. 4:1-4); for the truth shall make us free!

Many contend that even though these images, symbols, and customs originated in pagan circles, they are not seen as, nor thought of, as pagan now. On the surface, this argument seems to ring true. Most people don't know that the Madonna and child is imagery associated with the mother-child cult of Egypt, nor do they know that Santa Clause is actually a demon. However in the Book of Acts we read:

Acts 17:29-30 "Forasmuch then as we are the offspring of God, we ought not to think that the Godhead is like unto gold, or silver, or stone, graven by art and man's device. And the times of this ignorance God winked at; but now commandeth all men everywhere to repent"

Did you get that? Before Jesus, God may have winked at such ignorance, but now ALL must come to repentance.

The following three paragraphs are from an article by Robert Heidler on "Messianic Gentiles", I believe they further solidify the information I've tried to convey in this text.

"Prior to the fourth century, the Church was a very "Jewish" institution. Its teachings were based on the Old Testament understanding of God. Its cornerstone was the Jewish Messiah, Yeshua (Jesus). For most of the first century, its Bible was the Tanach, the Jewish "Old Testament." The worship of the Church was based on the Psalms, with much singing, dancing and celebration. Churches regularly celebrated the Old Testament feasts, even as Yeshua and the apostles had...

Beginning in the fourth century, however, Church leaders, enamored with the pagan Greek philosophy of the day, attempted to purge the Church of its Jewish roots. Repeatedly, councils condemned the observances of the Biblical feasts. In their place they substituted "Christianized" versions of pagan Greek feasts. For example, instead of celebrating Messiah's death and resurrection in the context of the Passover as the apostles had, they used the feast of the pagan fertility goddess, Ishtar — thus the origination of the name Easter...

As we learn about the Jewish roots of our faith, we find passage after passage coming into clearer focus, with long-hidden significance revealed. Passages that made little sense suddenly spring to life. We gain a deeper understanding of our Covenant rights, and of how God desires to relate to us. Jews who come to know their Messiah are sometimes referred to as "completed" Jews. That's a good description. But I believe it's also true that when a Gentile Christian comes to know the Jewish heritage of his faith, he becomes a "completed" Gentile! Yeshua is not only the Savior of the world, but the Messiah of Israel — and our Messiah. By His grace, we have been made fellow citizens in that commonwealth. The more we know of that heritage, the richer and more complete we will be."[2]

This is essentially the "one new man" (Ephesians 2:15) message. If Gentiles would come to understand that their faith in Jesus is completely of a Jewish origin, and they would reject the influences of men and pagans; the Gentile church would get back to its Biblical roots and once again provoke the Jew to jealousy (Romans 11:11); for we would be practicing an Torah observant form of Judaism, the same type that Jesus and His disciples practiced.

Dare to Stand Out

Most of us are by nature conformists. We tend to want to blend into the crowd and desire not to stand out as different. Most cultures teach conformity to their children early and often, and this initial training remains with them throughout their lives. Those who stray from conformity are called "black sheep," and are regarded somewhat suspiciously by "normal" people. As adults, we feel similar peer pressure, but the stakes are higher. Now it is cars, homes, memberships, investments, salaries, résumés, benefit packages, and vacation destinations—not to mention all the latest toys, gizmos, and accoutrements. Not running with the in-crowd is can be just as devastating to an adult as it is to a teen; the subconscious desire to fit in is ever present. We may call it "staying in style" or "not wanting to fall behind," but it is the same urge not to stand out as different.

I must give you fair warning however, as giving up the traditional holidays may be one of the hardest things you do in your Christian life. You'll be standing against 1700+ years of false teaching; all of your friends and loved ones will still be celebrating these holidays, and you'll feel alienated from society during holiday seasons. Your family and friends will make fun of you, citing times in the past when you have celebrated their holidays, etc. You'll also be labeled a radical by your church leaders or be accused of converting to Judaism or even being legalistic. Being the black sheep isn't always easy, look at the life of Jesus and His disciples...

At this point, you've probably already fallen into one of three categories: 1) Your one that already shares and believes in the message of this book and have been waiting for such a text to show your friends and family you are in fact not crazy! 2) You are offended by this book because you so love your holiday traditions and refuse to believe evidence plainly put in front of you. 3) You've been blown away by this revelation and are still reeling from its impact on your theology...

If you are in the first category, bless you! I've been there and done that; keep going for your reward lies ahead and is not of this world. If you are in the third category- be encouraged for the Lord is calling you up to the next level of intimacy with Him! If you are in the second group, seek the truth for yourself and you'll no doubt come to the same conclusions, but should you refuse know that your heart is rocky ground and the relationship you believe to have with God is in fact no relationship at all.

We Christians have another ingredient to add to the mix: our calling. God's invitation to His Family really complicates matters in terms of fitting into society. He has called us out of this world (John 15:19). The purpose of His invitation is to make us different! If we accept His invitation, we agree to spend the rest of our lives as the proverbial sore thumb. We are set apart from other people in the world, and commissioned—nay, commanded—to widen the gap!

As I hear so often from my family members "Well each one has their own beliefs", as this is some sort of justification for their error and ignorance. "God knows my heart"- statements like these demonstrate the depth of deception one has fallen to. They're blind, deaf and lost...

Notice Paul's blunt statement in Romans 12:2: "Do not be conformed to this world, but be transformed by the renewing of your mind... ." John is equally as blunt: "Do not love the world or the things in the world. If anyone loves the world, the love of the Father is not in him" (I John 2:15). As is James: "Adulterers and adulteresses! Do you not know that friendship with the world is enmity with God? Whoever therefore wants to be a friend of the world makes himself an enemy of God" (James 4:4). And God Himself: "Come out of [Babylon, a type of the world], My people, lest you share in her sins, and lest you receive of her plagues" (Revelation 18:4).

Paul's warning in II Timothy 3:12 can be discouraging: "Yes, and all who desire to live godly in Christ Jesus will suffer *persecution*." The last of Christ's Beatitudes offers some balance: Blessed are those who are *persecuted for righteousness' sake*, for theirs is the kingdom of heaven. Blessed are you when they revile and persecute you, and say all kinds of evil against you falsely for my sake. Rejoice and be exceedingly glad, for great is your reward in heaven... . (Matthew 5:10-12)

Is this reason enough to dare to be different? I truly believe so; for I know that we will inherit the kingdom of heaven, and I know what we are doing is true to the word of the living God and because I have come to know Him through this refining process. We're called to be peculiar people (1 Peter 2:19), what makes us different from everyone else if we celebrate the same holidays and Sabbaths as the heathen? Nothing! That's why we must separate ourselves unto God.

Joshua 24:15 "But if serving the LORD seems undesirable to you, then choose *for yourselves this day whom you will serve, whether the gods your forefathers (church tradition)* served beyond the River, *or the gods of the Amorites(pagans),* in whose land you are living. *But as for me and my household, we will serve the LORD*". {Emphasis mine}

Author Bio

Jason Hunt is the founding president of the Kingdom Harvest School of Ministry and Apostolic Overseer of Kingdom Harvest Ministries. He holds an undergraduate degree in church ministry and graduate degrees in ministry and theology (M.Min. and Th.D.). He and his family; Robyn, Ethan, Sydnee, Lindsay and Daniel live in rural Bethlehem, Kentucky.

You can visit Jason's online at: www.kingdomharvest.us or www.khsm.us

Introduction

D&C: Dilation and Curettage is a gynecological procedure performed on the female reproductive system that involves dilating the cervix and inserting instruments to remove the lining of the uterus, while the woman is under an anesthetic. Curettage is performed with a curette, a metal rod with a handle on one end and a sharp loop on the other. It is a type of abortion, The World Health Organization recommends D&C as a method of abortion only when manual vacuum aspiration is unavailable. — *A-Z Managing Complications in Pregnancy and Childbirth by WHO.* Retrieved on February 20, 2006.

Except for a shoddy translation of the word Passover appearing as "Easter" in the King James Version in the book of Acts.

Quote from Frank Viola, author of "Pagan Christianity" regarding holidays from his website www.ptmin.org

Ibid

Chapter 1: Pagan Origins

Pagan and Christian Creeds: Their Meaning and Origin, Edward Carpenter: 1920, Public Domain

Ibid

The birth feast of Mithras was held in Rome on the 8th day before the Kalends of January, being also the day of the Circassian games, which were sacred to the Sun. (See F. Nork, Der Mystagog, Leipzig.)

This at any rate was reported by his later disciples (see Robertson's Pagan Christs, p. 338).

See Plutarch on Isis and Osiris.

Ancient Art and Ritual, by Jane E. Harrison, Chap. 1.

A discoloration caused by red earth washed by rain from the mountains, and which has been observed by modern travelers. For the whole story of Adonis and of Attis see Frazer's Golden Bough, part iv.

Cox's Myths of the Aryan Nations, p. 107.

Bhagavat Gita, ch. xi.

I Apol. c. 66.

De Praescriptione Hereticorum, c. 40; De Bapt. c. 3; De Corona, c. 15.

For reference to both these examples see J. M. Robertson's Pagan Christ's, pp. 321, 322.

The Zodiacal sign of Capricornus, iii.

Chapter 2: Origins of Easter

Pagan Origins of Easter, Article by David J. Meyer, Last Trumpet Ministries

Ibid

Gerald L. Berry, "Religions of the World," Barns & Noble, 1956

Ibid

Ralph Woodrow, Babylon Mystery Religion (Riverside, California: Ralph Woodrow Evangelistic Assn., 1966)

"The resurrection of Tammuz [Nimrod] through Ishtar's grief [Semiramis] was dramatically represented annually in order to insure the success of the crops and the fertility of the people... Each year men and women had to grieve with Ishtar over the death of Tammuz and celebrate the god's return, in order to win anew her favor and her benefits! [Homer W. Smith, Man and His Gods, p. 86, as cited by Woodrow, p. 157.]

Pagan Origins of Easter, Article by David J. Meyer, Last Trumpet Ministries

Controlled by the Calendar p 46, 47

A Rood Awakening, episode: Truth vs Tradition, Michael Rood

Francis X. Weiser, *Handbook of Christian Feasts and Customs* (New York: Harcourt, Brace & World, Inc., 1958), p. 211. Copyright 1952 by Francis X. Weiser.

Herodotus' History, Book 2, p. 109

King James Version of the Holy Bible

Ibid

Ibid

Ibid

Larry Boemler *"Asherah and Easter,"* Biblical Archaeology Review, Vol. 18, Number 3, 1992-May/June

Wisconsin Evangelical Lutheran Synod Q & A Set 15, *"Why do we celebrate a festival called Easter?"*

Chapter 3: The Easter Revolution

Encyclopedia Britannica, 11ᵗʰ Edition, pub. 1911, Easter article

Francis X. Weiser, Handbook of Christian Feasts and Customs (New York: Harcourt, Brace & World, Inc., 1958), p. 211. Copyright 1952 by Francis X. Weiser.

Constantine, To the Assembly of the Saints, Eusebius, Church History 9-10

Two Essays on Biblical and on Ecclesiastical Miracles, 3d ed., Lond., 1873, pp. 271 sqq.

The Conversion of Constantine and Pagan Rome, Oxford: Clarendon, 1948

Pontifex Maximus by N.S. Gill, About.com Guide: http://ancienthistory.about.com/od/socialcustomsdailylife/g/pontifexmaximus.htm

The Conversion of Constantine and Pagan Rome, Oxford: Clarendon, 1948

From Jesus to Christ: The First Christians, Frontline; PBS Production

W.H. Barber, "Constantine in Relation to Christianity," *Review & Expositor* 9.1 (Jan. 1912): 63-82

Jewish Origins of Christianity, Raymond R. Fischer, Olim Publications 2004

Ibid

Ancient Roman Empire History, Art. Christian Persecution

The Vatican, http://www.vatican.va/liturgical_year/easter/2003/catechism_en.html

A blue law, in the United States and Canada, is a type of law restricting activities or sales of goods on Sunday, which had its roots in accommodating Christian Sunday worship, although it persists to this day more as a matter of tradition.

The Code of Justinian, Book 111, title 12, law 3.

Commentary on the Psalms, in Migne, Patrologia Graeca, volume 23, column 1171

Chapter 4: Rites of Passage

Gerald L. Berry, "Religions of the World," Barns & Noble, (1956).

Encarta Encyclopedia- Origins of Easter

Ibid- Easter in the Western Church

Ibid

Michael J. Rood, "The Pagan-Christian Connection Exposed"

Layard's Babylon & Nineveh, p.343Priests

Easter: Its Story and Meaning by Alan Watts; Babylon, Mystery Religion, Ralph Woodrow; Calvin Tracts; Knox's History

Francis X. Weiser, Handbook of Christian Feasts and Customs (New York: Harcourt, Brace & World, Inc., 1958), p. 211. Copyright 1952 by Francis X. Weiser

Michael J. Rood, "The Pagan-Christian Connection Exposed"

Controlled by the Calendar p. 47, Remnant of God: Easter Section, Ezekiel 8:15-16

Houston Chronicle, February 21, 2001

Francis X. Weiser, Handbook of Christian Feasts and Customs (New York: Harcourt, Brace & World, Inc., 1958), p. 211. Copyright 1952 by Francis X. Weiser

On December 8, 2003 Pope John Paul II publicly prayed: "Queen of peace, pray for us! Confess the holy Ever-Virgin Mary, truly and properly the Mother of God, to be higher than every creature whether visible or invisible and does not with sincere faith seek her intercessions, as one having confidence in her access to our God."

Controlled by the Calendar p 46, 47

First Conference Abbot Theonas, chapter 30

Controlled by the Calendar p 49

Encyclopedia Britannica, Babylon Mystery Religion

Controlled by the Calendar p 45
The Encyclopedia of Religion, 1987, p 558, "Easter
Albert Pike, an Illuminati member, in his Masonic treatise
"Morals and Dogma"
Controlled by the Calendar p. 46

Chapter 5: The Spring Feast

1. Rabbi Hayim Halevy Donin, "To be a Jew", on the Responsibility of the Synagogues Today, p 188
2. Unlocking Prophecy: Jesus Fulfills the Seven Feasts of Israel, Copyright 1994 by Return to God, P.O. Box 159, Carnation, WA 98014
3. Judaism 101: Jewish Holidays, When Holidays Begin, http://www.jewfaq.org/holiday0.htm
4. Dr. Richard Booker, "Celebrating Jesus in the Biblical Feasts", p 36
5. Ibid, p 43
6. Brown, Driver, Briggs and Gesenius. "Hebrew Lexicon entry for Pacach". "The Old Testament Hebrew Lexicon".

Chapter 6: Resurrection Day

1. Edward M. Reingold, Calender Book, Papers, and Code, Calendrical Calculations, 3rd Edition, Cambridge University Press, 2008

Chapter 7: The Origins of Christmas

Catholic Encyclopedia, 1911 ed., article: "Christmas."
Webster's New World College Dictionary, 4th Edition, art. Mass

Ten Difference between the Reformation and Rome: http://www.reformationtheology.com/2008/12/ten_differences_between_the_re.php

Catholic Encyclopedia, 1911 ed., article: "Christmas."

Catholic Encyclopedia, 11th ed., art: "Natal Day."

Vatican II: The Conciliar and Post Conciliar Documents Session 13: Decree on the Eucharist, chap. 5, Denz 78, 1648

Edward Carpenter, Pagan & Christian Creeds: Their Origin and Meaning

Francis X. Weiser, *Handbook of Christian Feasts and Customs* (New York: Harcourt, Brace & World, Inc., 1958), p. 211. Copyright 1952 by Francis X. Weiser.

Rev. Jack Barr, Cults, Queen of Heaven, http://prophecyarchive.com/ray/barr-family.com/godsword/queen.htm

C.H.E. Haspels, The Highlands of Phrygia, 1971, I 293 no 13, noted in Walter Burkert, Greek Religion, 1985, III.3.4, notes 17 and 18.

The Encyclopedia of Religion. McMillan. 1987. Vol 2. Pg 59-61

Chris Dolan's, Orion, retrieved Jan. 8, 2010: http://www.astro.wisc.edu/~dolan/constellations/constellations/Orion.html

The Final Move beyond Iraq by Mike Evans, Interview with Isser Harel, Page 2

The resurrection of Tammuz [Nimrod] through Ishtar's grief [Semiramis] was dramatically represented annually in order to insure the success of the crops and the fertility of the people... Each year men and women had to grieve with Ishtar over the death of Tammuz and celebrate the god's return, in order to win anew her favor and her benefits! [Homer W. Smith, Man and His Gods, p. 86, as cited by Woodrow, p. 157.]

Chapter 8: Deck the Halls
A Dictionary of Symbols, by J. E. Cirlot

Jordan Maxwell, "Hidden Roots of Religion" pt. 27

A Dictionary of Symbols, by J. E. Cirlot, p. 267

Masonic and Occult Symbols Illustrated; Dr. Cathy Burns ; edition 9/2004

Frederick J. Haskins, Answers to Questions

About.com; www.paganwiccan.about.com "Yule"

Ibid

Ibid

This was something told to me by my former pastor when I first asked him about the validity of Christmas and giving gifts in December of 2003.

Bibliotheca Sacra, Vol. 12, pp. 153-155.

Webster's Dictionary: Incantation: A Ritual recitation of verbal charms or spells to produce a magic effect.

Wassailing: Woodlands Junior School, Hunt Road Tonbridge Kent TN10 4BB

American Heritage Dictionary, Incantation

For more information in Speaking in Tongues see "Tongues as of Fire" also by Dr. Jason Hunt.

Chapter 9: What about Santa Claus?
Pagan Claus: A look at Christian Symbols; W.J. Bethancourt, III

Ibid

H4K: Where does God fit in?Bes; Portland State University in Portland, Oregon

The History and Traditions of Christmas; unknown, Christmas, www.remnantofgod.org

Christmas, http://www.balaams-ass.com

Ibid

New Schaff-Herzog Encyclopedia of Religious Knowledge, art: "Christmas."

Chapter 10: The Unconquered Sun

Encyclopedia Americana (1944 edition), art: "Christmas."
Encyclopedia Britannica, (1946 ed), Mithra
Ibid

VATICAN CITY, (ZENIT.org)—"How is it possible to explain the unique character of Christ and of the Catholic Church to a Jew or a Lutheran, a reporter asked Cardinal Joseph Ratzinger, prefect of the Vatican Congregation for the Doctrine of the Faith, during a press conference to present the "Dominus Jesus" declaration, which is concerned, precisely, with the unique and universal salvation of Christ and the Church. Cardinal Ratzinger clarified that "we are in agreement that a Jew, and this is true for believers of other religions, does not need to know or acknowledge Christ as the Son of God in order to be saved, if there are insurmountable impediments, of which he is not blameworthy, to preclude it. However, the fact that the Son of God entered history, made himself part of history, and is present as a reality in history, affects everyone."(Interview by Zenit News Agency)

Chapter 11: The True Birthday of Jesus

Michael Rood, "The Pagan-Christian Connection Exposed"; This is the best simplified explanation of the birth of Yeshua that I have found in any text, I did not feel I could improve upon it, so I included the original authors commentary throughout the first ten paragraphs of this chapter.

Ibid

Ibid

Ibid

Ibid

Ibid

Ibid

Ibid

Ibid

Ibid

Dr. Jason Hunt, "Tongues as of Fire"

Eddie Chumney, "Seven Festivals of the Messiah"

Rabbi Yitzhak Kaduri Confirms Jesus is the Messiah, http://www.youtube.com/watch?v=d4CZLCDRVzc

Dr. Richard Booker, "The Shofar", Ancient Sounds of the Messiah, p. 27

Dan Juster, Th.D., "Jewish Roots", p. 204

Ibid, p. 205

Ibid, p. 208

Ibid

Chapter 12: Halloween

Pagan Roots of Halloween, CBN.com — (Excerpt from *The Facts on Halloween* by Harvest House Publishers)

Ibid

Ibid

Duckworth, George E (1976). "Pomona" in William D. Halsey. *Collier's Encyclopedia.* 19. Macmillan Educational Corporation. p. 232.

Wikipedia Encyclopedia/ All Hallows Eve

Ibid / Samhain

The New Encyclopedia of the Occult, John Michael Greer, art. Mabon

Wikipedia Encyclopedia / Souling
Wikipedia Encyclopedia / Guising
Ibid
Ibid
Wikipedia Encyclopedia/ Jack O' Lantern
Ibid
American Catholic, St. Anthony's Messenger Press
Roman Catholic Catechism, #2116

Chapter 13: St. Valentine's Day
The Catholic Encyclopedia, Saint Valentine
Wikipedia Encyclopedia, art. Saint Valentine
The Catholic Encyclopedia, Saint Valentine
Ibid
Dr. Cathy Burns, Masonic and Occult Symbols
Lupercalia: http://www.meridiangraphics.net/lupercalia.htm
The Catholic Encyclopedia, Saint Valentine
http://ancienthistory.about.com/od/socialcustomsdailylife/a/010908Lupercal.htm
Classical Mythology, 7th Ed., p. 769, art. Erotic/erotica/eratomania, also see cupidity page 768.
Encyclopedia Britannica, 11th Edition, art. Cupid
Classical Mythology, 7th Ed., p. 769, art. Faunus
The New Encyclopedia of the Occult, John Michael Greer, art. Pan
Alex Jones, Dark Secrets of the Bohemian Grove available at www.infowars.com
Dr. Cathy Burns, Masonic and Occult Symbols
About.com; http://atheism.about.com/od/springholidays/p/ValentinesDay.htm

Chapter 14: St. Patrick's Day

11th Edition Encyclopedia Britannica 1911 edition, Art. Saint Patrick

Ibid

Ibid

Ibid

Ibid

Wikipedia Encyclopedia, art. Ancient Order of Hibernians

Definition of "sign" as referenced by Dr. Cathy Burns in her book Masonic and Occult Symbols, could not locate actual Webster's volume used for this definition, however, definition is in line with Webster's New World College Dictionary, 4th Ed.

Dr. Cathy Burns, Masonic and Occult Symbols

Ibid

New Encyclopedia of the Occult, John Michael Greer, art. Elemental, p. 150-151

Tom Garvin: *The Evolution of Irish Nationalist Politics* Gill & Macmillan (2005)

Helena Petrvna Blavantsky, Isis Unveiled Vol. 1, See also: John Lash, The Seeker's Handbook: The Complete Guide to Spiritual Pathfinding, pg.262.

Ibid

http://www.answers.com/topic/sabbath-witchcraft

Wikipedia Encyclopedia, art. Peter Pan

Ibid, art. J.M. Barrie

Laurie Cabot with Tom Cowan, Power of the Witch: Earth, Moon, and the Magical Path to Enlightenment.

11th Edition Encyclopedia Britannica 1911 edition/four-leaf clover

Slogan from General Mills, "Lucky Charms" cereal product

Chapter 15: New Year's Day

Popular New Year's Resolutions on USA.gov

Michels, A.K. *The Calendar of the Roman Republic* (Princeton, 1967), p. 97-8.

Ibid

Old Father Time, www.novareinna.com/festive/oft.html

Classical Mythology, 7th Ed., Marriage of Sky and Earth and their offspring, see Cronus

Chapter 16: Where do we go from here?

Quote by Dr. Jason Hunt made Hanukkah 2008

Robert Heidler, art. "Messianic Gentiles", an unpublished manuscript

Manufactured By: RR Donnelley
Momence, IL USA
October, 2010